The
Enigmatic
Sailor

The
Enigmatic
Sailor

Memoirs of a Seagoing Intelligence Officer

Alan Peacock

Whittles Publishing

Published by
Whittles Publishing Limited,
Roseleigh House,
Latheronwheel,
Caithness, KW5 6DW,
Scotland, UK
www.whittlespublishing.com

Typeset by
Samantha Barden

ISBN 1-904445-09-8

Printed by
Bell & Bain Ltd., Glasgow

CONTENTS

———

SOURCES AND ACKNOWLEDGMENTS

———

The main source of this account is my own memory supplemented by personal documents as a rating and later an officer, such as the ratings Certificate of Service, the Certificate of Promotion to Sub-Lieutenant, and Wound-And-Hurt Certificate issued after action in the Channel in October 1943 and my Statement of Service in the Defence Records held by the Ministry of Defence. I was able to supplement my account by substantial help from the Naval Historical Branch of the Ministry of Defence, thanks to the good offices of Mr J D Brown, its Head until 2000, and his successor Captain Page. In particular, they were able to supply me with the summary of records of service of all the eleven ships on which I had served as well as a translation of the German account of Operation 'Tunnel'. I also consulted the Public Record Office on documents relating to operations in the Arctic, but these contain no reference to Y service activities in that theatre of war.

The standard work on the role of naval intelligence during WW2 is, of course, F H Hinsley, *British Intelligence in the Second World War*, 1988 together with various co-authors for specialist themes, including E E Thomas, who was our 'control' in the Home Fleet. This work includes several references to Headache and Y. Y and Headache branches in the Royal Navy grew out of the experience of RAF interceptors when it was discovered that not only the Luftwaffe but also E Boats operating in the Channel and Thames Estuary communicated with one another not only in simple code but conversationally. Hugh Sebag-Montefiore's *Enigma: The Battle of the Code*, 2001, describes in detail the role of the Royal Navy in the capture of cipher machines as well as providing excellent accounts of the problems encountered by Bletchley in passing information to the Home Fleet, notably in the operations associated with PQ 17 and the sinking of the *Scharnhorst*. It also contains an extensive bibliography. Paul Kemp's *Convoy! Drama in Arctic Waters* published first in 1993 and re-issued in 2002 as a Cassel Military Paperback offers a compelling narrative of convoy operations, making extensive use of both British official reports and those now available from Russian sources.

I must record my grateful thanks to Kathy Mountain for skill and patience in typing several drafts. Morton Andrews, my shipmate who appears in Chapter 5, has supported my efforts in a number of ways and it has been a great experience renewing contact with him after so many years. 'Jock' Snaith, an old friend and with a different kind of adventurous career as an RNVR Officer well worth the telling, has been a great help in checking on my use of naval jargon. The reproduction of a splendid signed photograph of Betty Grable has been kindly supplied by another old friend, Graham Bannock. Also a special word of thanks to Simon Blundell, Librarian of the Reform Club, for help in tracking down some important source material.

I owe a special debt to Sir Michael Howard CH CBE for his commendation of the book to the reader and also to Ms Libby Purves OBE and Rear Admiral George Ritchie CB DSC for agreeing to read it in manuscript form.

A special word of appreciation is due to Mr John Wallbridge for allowing me to reproduce his map from his own account of Operation Tunnel published by the Channel Islands Occupation Society, and also to its Secretary Mr W M Ginns MBE.

I am grateful to the Kryptos Society of the Reform Club and particularly to its Secretary Mr Arnold Rosen, for the opportunity to present some thoughts on naval intelligence to their members. This encouraged me to preface my narrative with a general account the 'Y' service's role in eavesdropping.

It is not necessary to read between the lines of the text to sense the crucial part played in the narrative by my wife, Margaret, who has reminded me that the use of the first person should be avoided where possible. It is for her, together with our children David, Richard and Helen that the book was written.

Preface

AN UNUSUAL TALE

———

Oldies reaching 80 years have to think very seriously about whether or not they should retail events of 60 years ago. Memory may not be up to supplying accounts of what happened to them and corroboration made difficult by the gaps in the ranks of those who shared in dramatic, sometimes harrowing, experiences of war. There can be no presumption that they have anything of interest to add to the rows and rows of memoirs of war in the Military Section of the book chains and public libraries. There are easier ways of gaining an appreciation of dramatic events through film and TV. Indeed, the Ancient Mariner and his 'glittering eye' can be screened without the yards of accompanying narrative. Why read a book, when the crucial moments in our past history, even if not available on film, can be simulated, perhaps supplemented by eye-witness accounts of famous triumphs and disasters?

However, my publisher knows the market better than I do and I am grateful that he has been willing to present this account of my early life. A new factor in the demand by the reading public and a particular series of events offer encouragement. The reading public is showing increasing interest in the origins of scientific discovery. The sea has played an important role in this, as witness the books on the voyages of Darwin, Joseph Banks and others. The achievement of ocean-going yachtsmen is put into perspective by reading about the vicissitudes of those who first devised the means for calculating longitude. The particular event which spurred me to write this book is closely tied to scientific endeavour, namely the revelation of the role played by the combination of mathematics, statistical inference, linguistics and language skills in breaking the German military codes, including those of the German Navy (Kriegsmarine) during the Second World War. As devotees of popular science literature, mystery novels and military history know, this work was carried out at Bletchley Park and remained until recently one of WW2's best-kept secrets.

In reading the memoirs of those engaged in this vital part of intelligence work, one cannot fail to be struck by the frequent references to the ignorance of those involved at the various stages about the specific contribution of their work to the conduct of war, from the wireless operators taking down messages to the forwarding of their decoded content to military authorities. The most likely explanation lies in the golden rule of intelligence that the operational significance of any information should only be distributed on a 'need to know' basis, otherwise, security could be endangered. As I know from being a one-time senior government adviser, the attempt to enforce this principle is still regarded as of cardinal importance within the Civil Service, though its application becomes increasingly difficult under public pressure to have access to what governments are doing and intend to do, particularly if information is being used that one has personally supplied, willingly or unwillingly.

Bletchley's activities impinged on naval actions in two ways. The first was to encourage efforts to capture German cipher and decoding apparatus used by the Kriegsmarine, particularly in U-boats. That is a separate story from mine. The second was in providing vital information on enemy intelligence procedures and practices which could affect particular naval actions and the protection of convoys, that is to say tactical situations where quick decisions had to be taken. The reason why this required special personnel at sea to interpret and use Bletchley material and with what effect will shortly be explained. Here all that need be said is that this function was carried out by seagoing personnel of the so-called 'Y' service who were trained to intercept enemy messages sent by speech (i.e. by radio-telephony – R/T for short) or by key using Morse code (i.e. by wireless-telegraphy – W/T for short). Such personnel had to include servicemen capable of interpreting decoded messages which could offer insight into the strength of enemy forces and their intentions.

However, solemn treatises on military history are not my cup of tea or ration of rum. An accident of war meant that my rites of passage to adulthood took the unexpected form of my becoming a seagoing eavesdropper at the sharp end, so to speak, of the Enigma trade and with an unusual tale to tell. It may help to know something of the background.

Why did eavesdropping on the enemy require to be seagoing? This cannot be obvious to those familiar with modern intelligence methods which include unmanned spyplanes (Chapter 1). What follows is a chronological narrative but with intervals of random introspection and analysis, which is what you have to expect from an aged professor. Thus Chapter 2 includes some 'pop' social anthropology of life on the lower deck of a destroyer. Becoming an officer, first working largely on one's own (Chapter 3) and then in charge of a group of specialised ratings (Chapter 4-6) offered an entirely different life. Whereas as an ordinary seaman on a destroyer one settled in and became a recognized member of a close-knit society following the predestined grooves of the North Sea convoy route, as a seagoing intelligence officer one was sent only on operations in Northern waters where 'Y' intelligence information could be crucial; in other words one would be likely to see action at almost every change of a ship's course. The only constant element in this marine nomadism, during which I served on no fewer than 11 ships, was the job itself; but the modes of operation and attendant excitements of the job offer a useful strand on which to base the narrative. Finally, appropriate though it might seem to end the composition when war ends, the interwoven themes denoting the sharing of experiences of extremes of danger, weather and boredom seem to call for a coda of sorts. It is well known that being a sailor marks one for life – it certainly increases one's vocabulary of colourful language! In my own case, it had a potent influence on my subsequent career in unexpected ways which may interest the reader (Chapters 7 and 8 and the Epilogue).

Chapter 1

THE RATIONALE OF EAVESDROPPING AFLOAT

———

As the story of naval intelligence during the Second World War has unfolded by the gradual release of official documents, the identification and interpretation of enemy radio signals are revealed as having been of major significance in naval actions. This first became clear in the case of Radar used to ascertain the position of enemy aircraft and ships. Radar was immensely important because it only took the presence of an enemy craft of some kind to be within a given distance for detection to take place and give the prospect of tracking its movements on a screen. However, while inferences could be drawn from Radar about future movements of enemy craft and their implications for the timing and nature of the action taken to frustrate attack, it could give no information on the intentions of the enemy and the enemy's appreciation of the opposition that it might face. In any naval operation some form of communication has to be established between the commanding authority and the participating unit if the objects of the operation are to be achieved. Additionally, any major operation needs to be supplied by the High Command – the Admiralty – with intelligence not otherwise available about enemy intentions with the necessity for clear and quick lines of communication by land line and wireless telegraphy. To frustrate enemy attempts to have access to this information, messages would need to be sent in code and the more sensitive the information the greater the necessity to make the code secure.

Both the sender and the receiver would require technical apparatus to encode and to decipher. The technical problem produced a trade-off between rapid communication by low priority messages encoded and deciphered quickly and high priority messages containing highly sensitive information which might take much longer to encode and decipher. Of course, as we all know from films about the war in the air, there would be circumstances where speed was so essential in winning battles that anyone able to listen in to communication between aircraft would hear what was almost ordinary speech garnished with slang. But the most vital pre-condition for making the system of intelligence work would be the removal of all temptation to those engaged in it to reveal what they were doing, thus adding that element of drama dear to the novelist and filmmaker if security were breached by the infiltration of spies or the passing of secret documents to the enemy. (I must confess that becoming part of these activities at the relatively tender age of 20 gave me a special feeling of self-importance!)

The mystery, romance and excitement attached to Bletchley Park is heightened by the drama arising from the formidable difficulties encountered in keeping up with German efforts to frustrate British deciphering activities by changing codes and using machines which complicated the methods of encryption. After WW2 the Germans were surprised to find that (despite these efforts) their Enigma system kept on being penetrated. However, the success of accumulating information by revealing the text of decoded messages and interpreting their meaning could be limited if some messages were not being intercepted. Coverage of German radio transmissions was achieved by radio receiving stations linked to Bletchley Park and, although extensive, 100 per cent coverage could not be guaranteed. Radio transmission was subject to interference from weather and distance in days when it could only be made terrestrially, that is to say before satellite transmission was possible. This was particularly true of messages sent from isolated and distant enemy transmitters in the Arctic, both shore-based and on board ships. Reception on the British mainland could often be patchy.

Whether this called for ensuring coverage of these blank areas depended on whether it would be of operational importance and whether personnel could be spared from other intelligence activities in order to conduct interception work at sea. What decided the matter was the demonstrable need for interception as part of the armoury of naval craft protecting the Russian convoys and therefore faced with attacks by both large surface craft such as the *Scharnhorst* and *Gneisnau* as well as JU 88 and 188 bombers and, increasingly important as the war proceeded, U-boats. Action to match the recognition of the problem was slow in coming and, as so often happens in war time, it took some awful debacle – in this case the fate of PQ 17 in 1941, the famous Russian convoy in which so many merchant ships were lost – to bring it about. The autopsy conducted by senior naval officers at the Admiralty and covering the 1941 convoys concluded that had intelligence information supplied by Bletchley been fully appreciated, the naval escorts would have been in a better position to protect the merchant ships from German attacks from the air and by U-boats. I may have joined the Navy to see something of the world but had no desire or expectation to find that reaching dry land meant stepping ashore at Scapa Flow at one end of the journey and a spell in an anchorage close to Murmansk at the other. This was to be my destiny in the last eighteen months of the European War.

A second problem was presented by the inevitable time lag between the receipt of signals and their availability to those acting on the information that they contained. This is still a general problem because of the organization of the process of selecting what is important and for whom, a task in which the Admiralty would be bound to take the lead. If the information on enemy intentions related to events some time ahead, then the time lag could be less important than in the case where it related to enemy decisions about the immediate future. The extreme case is represented by the use of communication by speech between enemy ships about to be or already engaged in action against British forces. Clearly, if signals could be picked up and revealed vital information of enemy intentions, then they would need to be acted upon immediately. This was the reason why after 1941, when coastal convoys were increasingly attacked by E-boats, destroyer escorts began to be manned by the so-called 'Headache' operators for intercepting R/T signals containing coded speech. In my own case, I was a rating operator from August 1942 to June 1943 on East Coast convoys running from Sheerness to Rosyth and back.

A third problem consisted in how to specify the skills necessary to perform the seagoing eavesdropping functions. In the case of R/T interception, which was employed against the enemy, notably in E-boats attacking convoys on the East Coast, directing their action required short speedy messages as for example in giving commands which were to be carried out immediately. This required that the interceptor and the interpreter of the message had to be the same person. Messages would be delivered in a primitive code as a form of shorthand. He would have to have good hearing, and sufficient knowledge of colloquial German to understand a message's contents. To be fully equipped linguistically, a general knowledge of German popular culture and even literature seemed necessary. When the pressure was on to find recruits to fulfil this highly specialised activity, it was necessary to recruit far beyond naval conscripts and the confines of nationality. Books and firms make much of the intriguing combination of high intelligence with alarming eccentricity found amongst the boffins of Bletchley but the eventual tally of 'Headache' operators, mainly on destroyers, would yield nothing to Bletchley in the colourful nature of their backgrounds and personalities. I recall meeting operators who were Czechs, Poles, Belgians and German (refugees) glad to be saved from internment and the Pioneer Corps and whose civilian occupations varied from teacher and literary scholar to Continental aristocrats probably mentioned in the Almanack de Gotha. It was said of them that they found it easier to hold ordinary conversation in the language of the enemy!

Where enemy signals had to be picked up by wireless-telegraphy (W/T) a demand for rather different skills was called for. This was the main method of communication over long distances, particularly when convoy operations and battles between opposing naval craft, including aircraft and U-boats were strategically important enough to require monitoring by the High Commands of either side. Messages would be sent out frequently and every hour of the day and to cover the radio frequencies it was necessary to have teams of telegraphists with special training in the procedures used by German transmitters. The decoding of messages which Bletchley did not receive or could not be sent out in decoded form quickly enough required the placing of officers attached to the staff of the commanders of particular operations who had to take overall responsibility for both the interpretation of the decoded messages and the management of the telegraphy team. Those like the author who found themselves transferred from R/T to W/T interception had to have special training which, for reasons explained later, was undertaken by the RAF intelligence services. Bletchley's task was the breaking of the daily ciphers and we were supplied with the results of this highly skilled activity which we applied to reading the messages taken down by our telegraphic teams – always provided that the necessary information could get through to us. Even if we were unaware as to how Bletchley obtained this information, we had the more interesting task of analysing the decoded messages to discover whether any of them were relevant to the particular seagoing operations on which we were engaged. As with R/T, constant changes in German signalling procedures designed to fox their enemies required us to be sent ashore for short periods of re-training.

The presence of 'Y' services officers and ratings in areas where interception of enemy signals was strategically important could be regarded as a victory for the Signals Division of the Naval Intelligence Department. That division organised recruitment, training and placement and presumably had the power to persuade the top brass in each naval Command to place the personnel where they were needed. There was certainly an element of uncertainty about how successful they would be in supplementing other sources of intelligence, and the chance was being taken that somehow 'supply would produce its own demand'. This last problem is illustrated particularly well in the case of smaller ships such as destroyers. Taking crew on board as ratings engaged on intelligence work presented a security risk and something other than having them sign the *Official Secrets Act* would be required to prevent too much talk about what they were doing. A partial solution arose because interception of R/T signals was not continuous. The ratings could not be left to hang about doing nothing in periods of non-transmission of signals, which would be a potential cause of trouble with, say, gunnery crew members who also performed mess duties and scrubbed decks and painted ships in harbour. The problem was complicated by the status of 'Y' ratings who were given the equivalent of Leading Seaman rank with expected promotion to Petty Officer. The only exception was the case of those ratings who had been marked out for possible promotion to officer and who had to serve time at sea as Ordinary Seaman. A common solution was to employ 'Y' ratings as Ship's Writer to perform secretarial and office duties, being persons of some education. In my own case, being a candidate for a commission I had to be treated as an Ordinary Seaman, but became Navigator's Yeoman responsible for keeping the ship's charts up-to-date. This exempted me from some but not all of Ordinary Seaman's duties, but kept me on the pay of the lowest rank.

I doubt if destroyer captains on the East Coast convoys could have forecast what a curious bunch of ratings would join them as 'Headache' operators. Of different ages, nationalities and temperament but generally cultured and well-educated, they presented a potential difficulty in becoming assimilated, and might even be a disruptive influence. My own experience is detailed later but I do remember one instance when the Admiralty promulgated a scheme by which graduates on board ships could be invited to give talks on current affairs and I volunteered. I was questioned at some length by a worried First Lieutenant who equated economics with revolutionary Marxism. More amusing were the stories about 'Headache' operators trying to familiarise themselves with reporting procedures to the captain on the bridge. Anyone with a cinema or TV education will have observed that naval commands and their acknowledgement have to be crisp and accurate. The case of Leading Writer S…vitch orginally from Central Europe was a common source of merriment. Reporting to the bridge, he adopted an original phraseology: "Good morning Captain, Sir. I hope you well. I watch for enemy and will be at your side until I am reliev-ed by my friend". In the case of R/T interception, the areas where it could be important were well specified, notably the Channel and the North Sea and there were well-prescribed routes followed by naval craft. (Of course, curious things could happen. One 'Headache' crew was placed on a destroyer in Home Waters which was suddenly sent to the Caribbean, not an area where their talents could be usefully employed. Only when some months later, the destroyer was sent to Simonstown, S.Africa, was it possible to disembark the 'Headache' crew. They were placed aboard a troopship which was sunk off West Africa on the homeward journey. Their adventures continued. They were picked up by a U-boat and landed in French West Africa where they languished in jail until liberation resulted in their release. They had been out of the operational area for 'Headache' for nearly two years. One of these unfortunate men later became a Petty Officer 'Headache' man on a destroyer sunk on the Russian convoys but survived that ordeal as well.)

In the case of operations where enemy W/T signals were the source of intelligence, a different set of circumstances prevailed. The complement for interception work no longer consisted of two operators but two officers, in some instances one of them non-commissioned, with a team of a dozen or more ordinary or leading telegraphists. While at sea they would have to keep continuous watch but only be required for specific operations and these could be anywhere in the North Atlantic and Arctic, but particularly near the Norwegian coast, including Spitzbergen. Their efficient deployment and the maintenance of security was achieved by attaching them to a shore station and assigning them to a separate location, usually a large Nissen Hut. They could then be quickly mustered and placed aboard the naval craft from which the Flag Officer in charge would direct operations. With the Flag moving from ship to ship, this obviated the necessity for particular ships having to include a complement of 'eavesdroppers'. This arrangement had some interesting repercussions. Our crews became a closely-knit community, reinforced not only by close contact at sea but also travelling together from our 'refuelling base' in Cheadle, Staffordshire, where re-training periodically took place. But, disguised as shore-based sailors for purposes of pay and leave and told to keep their mouths firmly shut about what they were doing, there was difficulty after the war in convincing the naval authorities that they had done a considerable amount of sea-time and were therefore entitled to appropriate decorations.

The above account may give the impression that it was based on some background information issued to intelligence officers on taking post. Nothing could be further from the truth. I recall when my dear father became the first government entomologist appointed by HM Government in 1910 to investigate the causes of malaria in Nigeria – then known as the White Man's Grave – that all he had by way of guidance was a short personal letter of advice from the famous tropical medicine expert, Sir Patrick Manson. When opting under initial naval training to apply for the 'Y' service no officer in the Royal Navy could give me any idea about what would happen to me. Even after special instruction, all one had left in one's hands was a code book and a diagram of a V(ery) H(igh) F(requency) radio receiver. But like Houseman's *Shropshire Lad* I was young and foolish – and not even yet one-and-twenty – bent on a course of action which might lead to a more interesting life than the majority of fellow naval recruits. At least that part of the story became true but not in the way I expected.

Chapter 2

THE LOWER DECK

———

The call to arms

When on 3 September 1939 Neville Chamberlain announced that we were at war with Germany, my father told me to forget about going back to Dundee High School to add some subjects to my rather poor Leaving Certificate and to enter university as a non-graduating student. I was 17 and the call-up age would be likely to be reduced quickly to 18. It would not have occurred to him to recommend that I should follow the example of my slightly older school contemporaries and volunteer.

There was a reason for this. My father and mother, Alexander and Clara Peacock, had had strong pacifist leanings. This was not surprising. Alexander Peacock, a Lecturer in Zoology at Armstrong College, Newcastle-upon-Tyne joined the RAMC in 1915 and was a stretcher bearer in the First Battle of the Somme, and later, when made an officer (very unusual for a non-medical), served in the Trench Fever Commission. He was equally horrified by the losses from enemy guns and from the debilitating effects of disease. Like so many others, he believed that such horrors must not be repeated and regarded it as his duty both to oppose militarism and to make friends with the enemy. My mother was just as committed to this view. It affected Joan, my sister, and I at an early age for our parents took us three summers running to Germany, for the first time when I was 5 and my sister 9. By then my father was Professor of

Zoology at University College, Dundee – a college of the University of St. Andrews – and had common research interests with German scholars; and we could live comfortably and modestly in German Gasthöfe for some weeks in the summer for very little, but this stopped when Britain left the Gold Standard in 1931. We had two German au pair girls, Hedi and Greta, in successive years, and my sister, Joan, on leaving school in 1936, spent six months with a German family in Saxony. By then the Nazis were becoming all-powerful and my father altered his views when a German schoolmaster friend began sending him Nazi propaganda.

My parents' idealistic principles had an important effect on my school career and subsequently on my choice of war service and even on the war service itself. They wanted me to learn German and fortunately the teaching at Dundee High School was excellent, a fact I did not realise until I joined Naval Intelligence. There was nothing unusual in that, as it had remained the second foreign language at school. What did make for awkwardness was the firm refusal of my parents to allow me to be enrolled in the school Cadet Corps which prided itself on its connection with the local regiment, The Black Watch, and which some masters regarded as a useful complementary way of improving school discipline. However, I cannot say that it seemed to worry 'non-joiners' provided it did not divide one from one's friends, and there was some relief at not having the school's hold extending into the summer vacation in the form of a Corps Camp. When war came, those of us without some military training were therefore not pre-destined, as it were, to enter the Black Watch or perhaps the Fife and Forfar Yeomanry. True, one might be rather envious of those members of the Cadet Corps who were immediately granted commissions and could impress the girls with their splendid Highland dress. (Later one had guilt feelings when some were lost or taken prisoner at St. Valery covering the retreat to Dunkirk.) However, at least one was more aware of the options open so long as a choice of how to serve remained.

It was well before I was due to be called up that I decided to join the Royal Navy. I cannot offer a fully satisfactory reason for doing so, even to myself. The traditional glamour attached to the Senior Service was still prevalent. I had enjoyed sea trips as a boy, one with my parents on a Japanese cargo boat which made a convenient stop at Marseille as my father wanted to visit the University of Montpelier, and two schoolboy cruises to the Baltic and Norwegian Coast on a troopship. (Sea travel was amazingly cheap in the 1930s and a 14 day schoolboy cruise cost only £6 per head, all found.) By 1940 my parents, who had now become deeply committed to the war effort, took very kindly to the idea of my choosing the Royal Navy, in particular my mother who envisaged convoy duty as less likely to develop the harsh militaristic qualities associated with soldiering, and, so she believed, likely to be less dangerous.

By my second year at University it was compulsory to enlist in some form of service training and, as there was no university naval division, I joined the Senior Training Corps. My attempt to adopt a low profile was out of keeping with my competitive spirit and I actually passed my Certificates A and B in the minimum time and found myself promoted to Sergeant. I kept quiet at home about my military progress and particularly about the acquisition of some skill at bayonet drill at which the main recommendation of the Black Watch Sergeant Instructor was to 'aim for their goolies'. It probably had not occurred to my mother that basic training in the Royal Navy would likewise include an introduction to combative skills, as I was soon to discover.

Boarding the *Stone Frigate**

I was called up to join the Royal Navy in April 1942, being lucky enough to be granted deferment to allow me to complete a War Degree in Economics and History at the University of St. Andrews the month before. I had to move quickly to meet the date of my entry into the Royal Navy, hastily bid my parents and close friends farewell, held an auction of a few possessions in my room in St. Salvator's Hall, St. Andrews and made for Edinburgh and the overnight train to Doncaster where, after a change at some godless hour in the morning, I could expect to reach HMS *Royal Arthur*, Skegness, at the appointed time. I had the choice of three trains and chose the last one which would get me there on time, so that I could treat myself to a visit to the cinema in what was then to me The Big City. Many others must have had the same idea, because the last overnight train was packed with a variegated assortment of service men and women, the cheerful going on leave and the sombre returning from it, and, all it seemed, fortified by drink and clutching what they had been

---

[*]Naval Jargon of this kind is defined in the Glossary and denoted by an asterisk.

able to muster in the way of war-time fare. Clearly, escape into slumber was out, though I couldn't do other than envy the sergeant who lay on a table in the pose of the sculpture of The Dying Gladiator and slept (and snored) for hours. We chugged along – Berwick, Newcastle, Durham, Darlington appeared and disappeared – and then we stopped dead somewhere between Northallerton and Thirsk, and remained there for 10 hours. It was the night that York was subjected to a Baedeker air raid, and the earlier train I might otherwise have taken was wrecked in the bombing – my service career might never have begun at all. My arrival at the gates of HMS *Royal Arthur*, hungry and exhausted, was after the prescribed time of reporting, but the Naval Police were gratifyingly unconcerned. "We only goes a'ter the sprogs* if they don't make it within a week" – so I was not put on a charge.

I was the first member of my generation in our family to join the services since my father and his two brothers had returned from World War 1, but already my father's youngest brother, my uncle Basil, a Major in the Territorials and a prisoner in WW1, had been captured in Singapore and taken to the river Kwai. (He survived and wrote a splendid book about his experiences.) So there was some interest in my fate, which gave rise to a further incident. My dear 80 year old grandmother was inconsolable and wept for days on hearing that I had joined the Royal Navy. Her worries, however, turned out to have nothing to do with concern for my safety. I had brought disgrace on the family. It took some time to discover why. In her youth, the Navy was supposedly the refuge of those who had run away from home, often to avoid being faced with a paternity order. I don't think that she ever came to believe that her eldest grandson was innocent.

As C/JX 357249, my Port Division was Chatham, which I never saw as a rating, and then only for one day as an officer in transit who was sent a bill for lunch for some derisory sum months after my demobilisation. There was little of the naval dockyard about HMS *Royal Arthur* which was Billy Butlin's famous holiday camp commandeered for the duration. Although the chalet beds were partitioned so that two ratings could share a rather narrow bed, and we were not there to be entertained by concert parties, a vestige of the camp atmosphere lingered. Surrounded by the (unheated) swimming pools and the now tatty decor of what had been the bars and restaurants, it was difficult to believe that one was going to be trained to face formidable enemies.

I was better prepared for initial training than many for much of it was taken up with square bashing. I was also in the peak of physical condition having been captain of the University Cross-Country team. The privileges of being a scion of the professional middle class paid off in my having travelled a good deal, often on my own, and it was a revelation to discover how those less fortunate had often never left their village or town and had to fight homesickness.

I had no difficulty settling down and became horribly complacent. A couple of weeks after arrival I romped home first in a cross country race over pancake-flat Lincolnshire in what was considered record time. Our Divisional Officer offered me a morning off to recover. After STC training the simulated menace in the voice of the drill Petty Officer had no terrors for me. "Some of you may thinks I'm mad", he shouted, fixing his eye on some quaking rating. "I'm the only one here who can prove 'e's sane". He pulled out of his pocket a piece of paper. "I've a certificate to prove it". He led us to believe it to be the certificate of release from a mental asylum. The IQ tests, the lectures on seamanship and practical instruction on knots and handling of ropes, the races up and down the practice rigging came easily. As I had hoped and had been led to expect, I was marked down as a CW candidate*, that is to say that I was regarded as potential officer material. So I was to be diverted from the basic training of an Ordinary Telegraphist and would train as an Ordinary Seaman, and do the necessary sea time and, if I did not get into trouble (including being lost at sea), I would qualify for officer training and become a Temporary Acting Sub-Lieutenant, but in view of my eyesight, not a watchkeeping officer.

Along with three others, issued with bag and hammock and a small brown case – the successor to the *ditty box* – and after only a month in bracing Skegness I set course for Fareham, Hants, and HMS *Collingwood* where we were to continue our training. Then my troubles began.

HMS *Collingwood*

Admiral Collingwood was a great name to my Northumbrian forbears and one imagined that his shade would protect his own kind in the rites of passage to become a sailor. One did not expect that the almost avuncular approach to that process at *Royal Arthur* would prevail in what was rumoured to be a strict training school, but the shock of change was electric in intensity. One had only to go through the gate for the first time to observe that there was nothing benign in sight, except the presence of a few nice-looking Wrens,* although they, too, presented the aura of soulless efficiency in their bearing and looked down their noses at the rather nervous new arrivals.

It was soon clear that I would have to conquer my impatience and control my mischievous tongue more than usual because of two unexpected happenings. The previous initial training at *Royal Arthur* was disregarded and the CW candidates were lumped together with the new entrants to begin square bashing and elementary seamanship all over again. This was infuriating and even raising the matter with the DO (Divisional Officer) was regarded almost as an affront to the establishment which still regarded *Royal Arthur* as a mere holiday camp. Worse still, the unit in which I found myself consisted of some really rough Cockney characters who were to take unkindly to being brought into line with naval discipline. They had all the resilience associated with their kind and could be most entertaining, but, as a unit, we were marked down as needing particular attention. Collective punishment in the form of extra drills and fatigues were used to sort us out, though this seemed to incite a small number of them to try to take the micky out of the Petty Officer in charge of us. It was difficult not to laugh when one of them deliberately dropped his rifle, exclaiming to the instructor: "Sorry, Chief, but I suffer from me corns." I recall 'Ginger' who was always in trouble of some sort. He was a clubbable and engaging companion off the parade ground, full of wonderful stories about his chequered career, but it was difficult for us to protect him from the wrath of authority. He confessed to me that he had deserted from the Army because he had undergone so much punishment drill. When he sensed that the Army was closing in on him, he avoided capture by volunteering for the Navy, and so far the bureaucratic process had failed to detect what he had done. I never found out what happened to him and hope his luck held.

I, too, was soon in a bit of trouble. A few days after arrival I was cook of the mess, which entailed responsibility for the safe return of crockery and cutlery after meals. An argument broke out amongst a few of my Cockney confrères and in the ensuing rough-house several saucers and plates crashed to the deck. My fellow cook and I, entirely innocent, were placed on a charge. The next day we were solemnly marched down the length of the parade ground under guard, for summary justice could not be delivered by our Divisional Officer (DO) if the charge was likely to entail financial penalties. The judicial procedure took a whole morning, and we were finally arraigned before a four-ring Captain with the physiognomy of Mr. Punch. We smartly reacted to 'Off caps' and, bare headed, listened to the solemn reading of the list of crimes attributed to us. My account of events was brushed aside and we were weighed off with the deduction of the cost of the broken items from our pay and told to get a haircut. We were both immensely relieved because the criminal proceedings were mildly terrifying and seemed out of keeping with the trivial nature of the offence. When, as required, I reported to the pay office to have my fine recorded, a sympathetic Wren subverted the process of justice by some accounting subterfuge which reduced the claim on my limited resources. Shortly afterwards, we were to be issued with a cardboard disc denoting our religion, so that we could be allocated to the appropriate church parade on Sundays and also provide the necessary data for a burial service in the event of our demise. We lined up and the PO in charge barked at each in turn: "C of E, Catholic or Nonconformist?" My reply was "Church of Scotland". "Yer mean Nonconformist!". "No", I replied, "C of S is not nonconformist", and added incautiously, "when the King comes to Scotland, C of S is the established religion". "You cheeky bastard, I'll put you down as an Atheist and you'll f------g well peel potatoes on Sunday morning!" "Sorry Chief …Nonconformist". As it happened the Nonconformist padre (known as the sin bo'sun*) was a cheerful radical who constantly reminded us that a piece of gold braid on your arm or 'scrambled eggs' on an officer's cap was of no interest to God. I often wondered whether he had deliberately chosen as the recorded Introit for his Sunday service the famous 'Meditation' from Massenet's 'Thais', an opera whose heroine was a notorious *fille de joie*.

Such things were only minor annoyances and not unexpected, but something had to be done to relieve the tedium of routine and the limited opportunities for entertainment when allowed a few hours' leave but within the confines of Fareham, not noted for its night life or cultural ambience. My parents forwarded a letter from my Alma Mater inviting me to graduate at the end of June or beginning of July, which was clearly not in prospect – but was there not just a chance I might swing this one? I filed a request for 'compassionate leave to graduate'. The DO looked doubtfully at me, but passed the request up the line to his Lieutenant-Commander superior. This is the end, I thought, for he seemed knowledgeable about such things. "Can't you graduate by proxy", he enquired. "No sir, only *in absentia*", I replied, truthfully. He hesitated and then added me to the list of 'requestmen' so that once again I would spend a whole morning going through the elaborate process which would lead me to face Punch again, only this time, I was put in charge of the defaulters and told to march them towards their fate. Eventually I appeared before Punch, this time saluting smartly but with my cap on. The request caused quite a stir, but the assembled entourage, some of whom clearly knew I was trying to pull a fast one, left it to Punch to ask the questions. "Who's graduating?" he sternly enquired. "Me, sir" I said as confidently as I could, fully expecting to be denounced by his staff. "Three days leave granted – about turn, double march". I just made it to the graduation and a dispensation was given to graduate in bell bottoms rather than full fig, and made it back in time. I reported, as required to the Master of Arms* who smiled, winked at the Regulating Petty Officer* and said "You're a sharp one – don't you try anything like that again!"

As training proceeded, there would be the occasional announcement at morning Divisions about the opportunities to volunteer for various branches of the Service. The PO in charge would preface the announcement with the word: "The following 'ave passed the trick cyclist's hexam which means they can volunteer for training as ...stoker ...signalman etc." To my amazement I found myself pronounced psychologically fit to train as a Petty Officer Motor Mechanic, and, barely able to handle a screwdriver, I remained silent. Some time later, I treated myself to the comfort of the saloon bar in a Fareham pub and found myself talking to a civilian whom I recognized as the base psychologist. How, I enquired, could I possibly have survived his scrutiny to be classified as a potential technician. He looked around him and took me in a corner. "It's really quite simple. The Admiralty sends us a request for so many MMs – their survival rate is low these days with the loss of so many Motor Torpedo Boats (MTBs) – and we simply pick out anyone with the equivalent of Matric who isn't clearly crazy".

Then one day I was summoned by the DO who, spotting that I had studied German at University for a year, showed me a Fleet Order requesting information on ratings with knowledge of German or who might be suitable candidates for the study of Japanese. He was not sure what the 'Y' service was, save that it came under the heading of Naval Intelligence. I let my name go forward, it being confirmed that I was still a CW candidate, and within days I was ordered to proceed to the Admiralty for interview, in the official expectation that I would not return. This proved to be correct and my transfer to HMS *Pembroke* was a cover for my reporting to RNTE (Royal Naval Training Establishment) Southmead, which turned out to be a large detached house close to Wimbledon Common. My hasty departure meant that I was deprived of the joys of instruction in gunnery, for what would have been at least three months' training at *Collingwood* had been cut to seven weeks. I imagined that I would be spending at least six months learning a mysterious trade. In fact I was doing sea time on a destroyer in less than a month from leaving Fareham.

The bell-bottomed graduate with parents – Professor Alexander Peacock
and Mrs Clara Peacock

A short sojourn in Suburbia

In the course of 1941, there had been several daring attacks on convoys off the East and South Coasts of England by German E-boats (Schnellbooten), and unbeknown to me, one which had caused consternation by sinking ships in Lyme Bay just about the time I left Collingwood. It was known that E-boats communicated by radio telephony (R/T) on VHF. For the officer commanding the boats to communicate orders rapidly, a low grade Code had to be used, and, if the R/T signals could be picked up, and could be quickly interpreted, naval craft defending ships in convoy would have warning of attack and might be able to forecast the tactics and numbers of the E-boats.

By then the now-famous 'Enigma' system was providing masses of information about German naval movements. The code crackers were able to compile a handbook of low grade code signals, which were principally based on German naval commands in abbreviated form. For example: "*AKV mit Ausführung – Frage Verstanden – Fertig*" rapped out by the command, meant "Full steam ahead – *(A)usserste (K)raft (V)oraus* – Understood? – out". To which the reply would come back swiftly: "*Verstanden*" (Understood). The number of replies could indicate the number of E-boats comprising the German fighting patrol.

Bletchley had a problem in exploiting this information. VHF signals could only be picked up at short range, and, even if Bletchley were supplied with them quickly, the delay in conveying the information in the coded messages could be too long to make it of any use to convoy escorts. The solution was to train naval personnel who knew German in German naval R/T procedure and to place them on board Royal Navy craft likely to engage E-boats or other craft, such as German destroyers, using the code. Hence the hurried establishment of what was called the 'Headache' branch of the naval 'Y' service, part of Naval Intelligence.

Those of us joining RNTE Southmead could only be dimly aware of the background to the revelation that they were going to be rushed through a process resembling a rapid results course in shorthand and typing and sent to ships likely to run into trouble. The fact that the work was 'hush-hush' and entailed the exercise of one's brains and memory offered a tinge of glamour and excitement during initiation, including the solemn reading out of the *Official Secrets Act*.

I survived the course – just. It was not difficult to grasp the essentials of radio communication and to learn how to search for wavelengths, the instruction by a very relaxed civilian radio engineer being excellent. I could manage to mug up the main German coding signals, though this fully tested my German vocabulary. The problem was that I had been well taught in literary German, once having actually been awarded an Alpha Minus for an essay written in that language on *Egmont als dramatischer Held* (Egmont as a dramatic hero). Unlike the other trainees, I had never held a sustained conversation in the language. Some of them were almost bi-lingual, and the only other Brit had lived in Germany. As already mentioned, those who came from countries in occupied Europe and had found their way to Britain, were glad to exchange life in the Pioneer Corps for something more in tune with their considerable skills. They were also much older than I was.

The course culminated with several simulations of E-boat communication in code with the added hazard of varying the strength of the signals to add a further touch of realism. Sometimes a brief conversation in German naval slang would be interpolated. I was often defeated by the problem of guessing the content of a signal corrupted by 'bad' reception, my hearing not being perfect and my colloquial German vocabulary being limited. Transcription of signals was another difficulty and one had to invent a personal shorthand to overcome the speed of delivery. I suppose that, desperate to match a limited supply of Headache operators to the excess demand, I was passed as fit.

The speed of my passage through the course can be gathered from the fact that I was on the complement of RNTE Southmead for only 18 days. I can hardly recall the names of any of those with whom I came into contact, and all that remains in my memory is the sweat and toil, but also the exciting challenge, of learning a new skill and the falsification of expectations about the opportunities to visit old haunts in Bermondsey where I had spent the summer of 1941 working in a social settlement, to hear some music again and perhaps to find somewhere to go dancing.

Two of us were supplied with a draft note to HMS *Wildfire*, the naval HQ at Sheerness, where the escorts of East Coast convoys anchored, my companion being a rather rotund and learned Polish refugee, double my age, whose German was better than his English. There was an understandable look of resignation on his face, and no great desire to communicate his thoughts. A truck dumped us with our bags, hammocks and small brown cases at Charing Cross station. We parted company at Sheerness and I never saw or heard of him again.

The journey to Sheerness started badly for me. I went to the Charing Cross booking office to exchange my travel warrant for a ticket, leaving my belongings close by. When I returned to pick them up, the case had disappeared. I would be joining my first ship completely depersonalised, for the case included my pay book, the loss of which was sufficient to put me on a charge, personal letters, clean collars and underwear, and toilet bag. My only means of identification was the disc worn on a piece of string round my neck with my official number C/JX 357249 on it. I was no longer a person but a cypher.

The Snakecharmer of HMS *Woolston*

An East Coast convoy was protected by a combination of daytime air patrols from shore bases and a brace of destroyers, the majority of which were of a rather ancient vintage. They included several four funnellers 'gifted' by the USA, which occasioned the splendid crack of Bernard Shaw who, on a visit to the USA during the war, said that he offered some of his old plays as an exchange for his hosts' generosity in supplying us with their old ships. They had a bad reputation for breaking down and for pitching and rolling sufficient to make even the most hardened tar seasick. The other old craft were V and W destroyers, constructed in WW1, I being assigned to one of them, HMS *Woolston*. They had also been adapted to modern warfare by installation of 4 x 4ins guns in twin mountings, 2 x 2ins "pom-poms" on single mountings and 4 x 20mm Oerlikons as well as 2 depth charge throwers. This armament was supplemented by various forms of detection of enemy surface and underwater craft such as RDF (radar) and Asdic (sonar) and, of course, 'Headache'. The net result of this modernisation was to increase the ship's crew by something like 50% above the peace-time complement, without, however, increasing the size of the crew's quarters. As compensation for the evident discomfort, an Ordinary Seaman (O/S) was paid an extra 6d per day as 'hard-lying money', considered by Lady Astor, MP for Plymouth, as over-generous and which she endeavoured to have stopped. She based her case on her experience of having once spent a week before WW2 on a destroyer in the South China seas, but not, so far as is known, on the lower deck.

As I was still a CW candidate, I had to forego transfer to the Writer Branch and promotion to Leading Writer, so I joined the ship as the lowest of the low, an Ordinary Seaman (H.O.) who had done no sea time. I had heard rumours that I would have to face some form of barbarous initiation ceremony and this thought, and loss of my personal gear, made me fear the worst. The Coxswain* was more amused than annoyed at my predicament, merely pointing out that I would be likely to receive the cold blast of a 'North Easter' at my first pay parade – the term being the graphic naval translation of the official jargon of being 'Not Entitled'. He shook his head sadly when I opted to be 'G' rather than 'T', meaning that I preferred my daily ration of Grog* rather than be classified as 'Temperance' which entitled me to 3d per day in lieu – what was a boy of my 'class' doing going down the well-worn path of perdition followed by 'common sailors'? I was appalled by his snobbery, but I was soon to learn that he was a first class seaman and a sympathetic source of support for anyone in trouble.

There was no ritual of induction. Everyone was too busy at sea and too anxious to get ashore when in port to spare the time for such shenanigans. The occasional practical joke entailed sending one on a fool's errand to ask an officer a stupid question. I soon learnt not to accept any invitation from the Chief Stoker to visit the Engine Room to be introduced to the 'golden rivet', that wonderful priapic symbol of the Lower Deck. The main requirement for acceptance was how quickly one could learn to pull one's weight and there I had some difficulties to overcome.

The first difficulty was that Headache duties did not involve continuous watchkeeping, but would normally be at night during the passage through 'E-boat Alley', roughly between the Thames and the Humber. That problem had been solved for my 'oppo', Denis Muschamp, who had become the ship's writer and could be fully employed. I was nominally an Ordinary Seaman, but one without any gunnery training and no recognizable technical qualifications to place me in the Engine Room, the Radar cabin or on the bridge. I landed a variety of dirty jobs from helping in the galley to being deputy 'captain' of the Heads*, i.e. cleaning the ratings' lavatory or colloquially the shithouse. The 'Captain' was a weary old sailor recalled, like several on board, from the Royal Fleet Reserve, who jealously guarded his rights and resented my presence, though content to allow me to clean the officers' heads, which was actually a slightly more congenial task. After some weeks, the drafting of a crew member left a vacancy as Navigator's Yeoman and, although I was unqualified, I knew something about maps, having a basic knowledge of cartography acquired in a university course on Geography. I was then made responsible for maintaining the charts in order and keeping them up-to-date by means of instructions contained in the monthly *Notices to Mariners* and was responsible to a very congenial RNVR two-ringer, the only menial task being to scrub the charthouse floor and polish its equipment. (The Headache man, Quaddy, on our sister ship, HMS *Wallace* was the ship's 'chippy' (carpenter), a skill he had acquired in his nomadic life as a kind of 'scholar gypsy' reminding one of the poet W.H. Davies.)

The next difficulty was common to all 'sprogs' going to sea for the first time in overcrowded vessels – where to sling a hammock. Denis Muschamp, as a Leading Writer, could sleep in the ship's office, which was reasonably comfortable, but, with the excess demand for hammock hooks and at the end of the queue, one had to have recourse to laying the hammock and blanket on the mess table, or on the lockers which served as mess seating or even under the table. In a calm sea or in harbour, under the table was safer and quieter, but the North Sea in winter is not very accommodating. The roll of the ship meant that you could only maintain a stable position by hooking your foot round the table stanchion and in a really rough sea – a frequent occurrence – the messdeck would be awash. When I became a 'Yeoman', I obtained permission to doss down on the charthouse deck, though one had to bring one's knees up to one's chin in order to fit in the limited space. It was several months before the great day came – one of the most satisfying in my life – when I had moved up the queue to acquire hooks of my own and could be lulled to sleep by the gentle swaying of the hammock induced by the motion of the ship.

But the main difficulty I faced was seasickness, which was entirely unexpected. This can make one very unpopular, not only because it is unpleasant to have a shipmate retching and sometimes not reaching the appropriate place to spew, but also because someone has to take over your duties if the doctor pronounces you unfit. To superstitious sailors – and many hardened 'salts' are – you are a bad omen and can become a pariah. On one occasion, lying prostrate in a hammock and assigned a hammock 'slot' belonging to someone else, I thought that I must be delirious when I discovered that a 'salt', with an evil glint in his eye, was shaving with a large carving knife the hairs of my arm drooping over the side of the hammock. Somehow, if slowly, I got my sea legs, and, no doubt without any scientific justification put my recovery down to acquiring a taste for neat rum. But perhaps the real reason was that I could not face the indignity of being put ashore, which would confirm the assertions of some of the more embittered 'salts' who had been hauled back for war service, that CW candidates – potential 'pigs' (as, regrettably, officers were sometimes called) – were the scrapings from the bottom of the manpower barrel.

Viewed from the perspective of the Lower Deck, life on board *Woolston* followed a distinct pattern. The expectation would be that going North, there might be trouble for the convoy in 'E-boat Alley' and that would mean watch-on watch-off – four hours on, four off – except for the 'dog watches' of two hours each, which gave a change-over of watch time for crew. There might also be a call to Action Stations when everyone would be called out. The 'Alley' was generally traversed at night time and by the second day the hope was that the convoy would be almost in sight of Spurn Head at the mouth of the Humber. From then on – we are talking about the autumn and winter of 1942-43 – there might only be occasional warnings of enemy action, perhaps an adventurous U-boat might be around or German aircraft bombing our cities might drop any remains of their load of bombs on the convoy as they returned home. If all went well, then we might reach the Longstone light before dark, and if we had St. Abb's Head on the port bow by dawn, we might be round the Bass Rock, might have left the convoy to be escorted into Methil, while we went through the Forth boom and under the Forth Bridge in time to tie up at Rosyth by midday. That would mean shore leave for at least half the crew, rapidly appearing at the 'liberty boat' parade impeccably dressed for inspection and, with a smart salute going over the side, would be off to savour the joys of the dancehalls, cinema, brothels, and pubs in the Big City – Edinburgh – or the more modest equivalents in 'Dunphers' (Dunfermline), the latter not to be despised with its excellent ice-rink where the girls paraded their charms in the revealing garb of skaters and its sybaritic Turkish Baths, bequeathed by its favourite son, Andrew Carnegie.

The same kind of expectations governed our trip South, with similar routines in reverse order. But there was one important difference. There was no joy on our faces at the prospect of swinging round a buoy at Sheerness, a place which in winter seemed to be enclosed in Stygian gloom, depressing to all but our Chief Gunnery Petty Officer who, rumour had it, was a bigamist with a family on the Isle of Sheppey close by and another tucked away near Dunfermline. I only remember one pub with any character – the Britannia Arms was it? – noted for its cheerful Renoiresque barmaids who gave as good as they got by way of chaff. However, lying in wait for us outside at closing time, ready to seize on us for being improperly dressed and spoiling for some sort of confrontation, were the villainous looking Naval Police seeking an excuse to put someone on a charge and who, barking at our heels, herded us back to the liberty* boats. I only remember one occasion when the trip across the oily waters of the Thames, as black as the River Styx, found us arriving aboard in cheerful mood. A very drunk and improbably looking Ordinary Seaman, but very portly and dignified, began singing in *basso profundo*, the famous Russian folk song *Stenka Razine*. With its short stanzas and catching melody, by the time we were halfway across, he had the whole liberty boat singing the chorus at the top of their voices.

Of course, expectations of the progress up and down the East Coast were not always fulfilled. We prepared for action every time we proceeded through E-boat Alley but it did not happen in my time. Denis and I spent hours searching for signals which were never sent, and calls to Action Stations, which were not infrequent, were false alarms. Our main enemy was the atrocious weather with rough seas and bitter cold, and it, rather than the enemy, frequently delayed our arrivals (and therefore our leave prospects) at the Forth or the Thames. Christmas Day 1942, for example, is engraved on my memory as the whole convoy lay at anchor off the Tyne in a pea soup fog. We were well supplied for Christmas Dinner and an unofficial dispensation allowed us to drink a lethal quantity of rum – which was not supposed to be stored up but consumed on the day of issue. By the end of the afternoon watch, exhausted by food, drink, raucous singing and other forms of contrived revelry, an uneasy silence seemed to descend over the whole convoy, and the ghostly forms of neighbouring ships resembled a kind of gigantic version of the set for Wagner's *Flying Dutchman*. Just occasionally one might hear the lone voice of a well-oiled sailor struggling to reach the high notes of some song expressing his yearning to be with his girl, a regrettable travesty of the *Helmsman's Song* at the beginning of that greatest opera of the sea.

Likewise, there was no way of knowing exactly whether or not our routine would have to be modified either by enemy action, a breakdown in the engine room of one of the merchant ships occasioning extra escort duty to see it into an unscheduled port, or simply the capriciousness of the 'cruel sea'. From time to time, we undertook an 'evolution' or exercise in which an enemy attack might be simulated. This was designed to test how alert we were, but it was interesting to observe that those 'evolutions' involving the firing of depth charges in response to the detection of a U-boat coincided with the identification of a shoal of fish. Large quantities of dead fish would be scattered in the wake of the ship and we would have a welcome variation in diet that day. This would also bring in our wake an extra army of gannets, ready to gorge on this unexpected feast. The old salts seemed to hate gannets which were rumoured, through transmigration, to embody the souls of departed Leading Stokers. A repulsive form of exorcism to remove the curse of their presence was employed. Fish surplus to requirements were caked in mustard and thrown back in the 'drink'* and the poor gannets who swooped down on this free meal were jeered as they choked and dropped the fish uttering a mournful shriek of horror.

These external constraints on our life could only be made tolerable if the ship's company had some power over their daily existence. Much has been written about the camaraderie of the Lower Deck, which offers a wonderful opportunity for the social anthropologist. I can only write about the personal experience of becoming tribalized. The 'sprog' was assigned to a mess consisting of a dozen ratings crowded into a small area dominated by the mess table anchored to the deck and with its own set of lockers and scuttles (port holes), the last-named being closed except in harbour. Each mess was in the charge of a Leading Seaman, who was responsible for the cleanliness of the mess and, what came as a great surprise, the preparation of meals for the mess. Scrubbing out the mess was normally conducted in harbour but sailors like anyone else expect to be fed at regular times. Every messmate had to take his turn as one of a pair of 'cooks' and serve for 24 hours. If lucky, the 'sprog' would be paired with an experienced hand, for sailors not only expect to be fed but fed well, and woe betide the cooks if their efforts were considered below standard. The cooks were given the raw materials for each meal, prepared them and presented them to the galley where the 'real' ship's cook supervised their translation into something hopefully edible. The first lesson to be learnt was that the ship's cook had to be enlisted as a 'friend' and that entailed occasional backhanders, notably in the form of sacrificing one's tot of rum. Messmates did not expect much variation in the main dinner course which would be determined by the meat ration – I remember masses of pork – which was far in excess of that then available to the civilian population. They paid particular attention to the quality of the 'afters'. Bread and Butter Pudding was regarded as poor nosh, and its hurried preparation by throwing currants into bread soaked in milk, earned it the name of 'tired man's duff'. You had to learn quickly how to prepare a steam pudding, if you wanted to earn the respect of your messmates. In addition to the acquisition of culinary skill, the mess cooks had to wash up after meals, and the state of the cutlery and plates after trying to get them clean in a limited quantity of hot water in a large dixie would be inspected carefully by the Leading Seaman. Being cook on a day when the sea was rough and 'Watch-on/Watch-off' was in operation was a test of concentration, stamina – and stomach.

The financing of the Mess revealed an interesting feature of judgment by one's peers. The individual mess was given a ration of 'essential' foods such as meat and flour and was also credited with a sum of money for other items normally purchased from the official store – the famous NAAFI. (The employees of NAAFI ashore had a rather poor reputation and were slanderously referred to as having No Ambition and F—- all Interest!) The mess was expected to spend the allocated sum but there was no registered objection to saving the money instead although there was one inhibition which limited this. Messes which saved and divided out the proceeds amongst its members were regarded as mean-minded and likely to end up providing poor fare. Considerable ingenuity was exercised by the more experienced hands in trying to keep up the catering standards whilst providing mess savings. They would use the funds to purchase from sources other than NAAFI and enter into sophisticated deals with dockyard contacts or with other ships. Here was clear evidence of Adam Smith's observation about the human propensity to 'truck and barter' to 'better one's condition' through exchange, recalling that Adam Smith wrote such words only a few miles to the East of Rosyth!

A sprog like myself would be lucky if he was apprenticed to an old salt and I was doubly lucky. After a rather miserable time in a badly run mess, I managed to get transferred to the same mess as my 'oppo', Denis. In civilian life he was a schoolmaster in Bristol, about ten years older than myself. He had taken well to his translation to sea dog, and his didactic experience, his height and presence commanded everyone's respect, particularly when, out of character, he would string some naval oaths together and remonstrate with some stroppy shipmate. He steered me several times through the shoals of despair when I was having a difficult time – about which more anon. The old salt to whom I was apprenticed as second cook was a West Countryman bearing up to the rigours of return to sea as a Reservist and already in his 40s. He was not only a good 'cook' and taught me, amongst other things, how to prepare steam puddings, but a shrewd observer of human nature who had a nose for any potential trouble, as, for example, when any of our number returned from shore leave the worse for wear. Although short and tubby and unable to square up to anyone in the mood for a fight, he knew exactly how to handle the fisticuffs brigade by the glint of an eye and the sharp edge of his tongue. No-one wanted to get across Alf Maple who was highly respected as a first class seaman, and a 'very present help in trouble' when a seaman needed intercession with a member of the quarter-deck, that is to say an officer.

The process of tribalization entailed something more than evidence that one was an identifiable cog in a war machine and able to perform the ancillary duties as cook in order to make life slightly more comfortable for all. One had to produce evidence of a distinct *persona* amongst the possible roles identified by the crew. Some were known for their physical strength, and others for being able to hold their drink; again others were skilled craftsmen who could carve wooden figures or produce leather work, useful sources of income, usually paid for by rum or tobacco. Still others were amateur comedians or musicians. The boatswain's* mate, for example, would pipe the Forenoon Watch and followed it by a sing-song 'Wakey, Wakey, rise and shine; the sun is scorching my eyes' – obviously the rain would be lashing down – and, after some of the crew had had a heavy night ashore he would add 'fish and chips for breakfast'. When piping 'Up spirits' for the daily issue of rum he would add the esoteric command: 'stand fast Queen Maud'. This was the invention of one of his forbears on the occasion when the coffin containing the late Queen of Norway was being conveyed from the UK to her final resting place by a naval escort. Clearly she was to be exempted from having to attend this important daily ritual.

I suspect that my talents were regarded as rather limited alongside such colourful characters. I had brought aboard a treble recorder which I could play reasonably well, but in those days it was rather a cult instrument associated with the strange practices of those interested in reviving ancient folk music. To warm my back I played it from time to time sitting next to the after funnel. It was our Captain, Lieutenant-Commander Hawkins, who christened me that 'bloody snakecharmer'. However, by accident, I hit it off with the tough lads, when they were short of a scrum-half to play rugby against HMS *Wallace* – rugby and not soccer being, surprisingly to me, the game of the Bristolians and West Country tars who formed a distinct group aboard. I had played at school and occasionally at university and was fairly nippy on my feet. I managed to score a try, and to prevent the 'Jimmy' (i.e. the First Lieutenant) of the *Wallace* from doing likewise by a lucky tackle. He was a certain Prince Philip of Greece. Twenty-two years later I had to accompany him on a royal tour of the University of York and thought it would divert him to recall this incident. I could not have been more wrong. His glare indicated that I had reached the height of impertinence.

The ultimate stage in becoming completely identified with the Lower Deck took an unexpected form. On a fateful occasion on shore leave, I took advantage of a standing invitation to visit some close friends of my sister who lived in North Queensferry, well within the permitted leave area, while most of my mates made for Edinburgh which was out of bounds. It was a great luxury to have a bath and then tea and a chat with Jimmy and Joey. (Jimmy

Smail was an accounting officer in the Dockyard.) In case of a sudden recall from leave, ratings were supposed to get in touch with Dunfermline Police Station before 6pm, but this was an instruction almost wholly disregarded. I had casually observed from the window of their house that two destroyers had disappeared under the Forth Bridge, but had not noticed their numbers. I went back to the Dockyard in good time for the 10pm curfew, and was stopped at the gate. "Was I from *Woolston*?" asked the Naval Police: "Yes" I replied. "Then you are under arrest". I was astonished: "What for?" "Missing your ship, and by Christ that means you're in trouble mate". I was marched under guard to what must have been the canteen during working hours, and spent an uncomfortable night on a palliase along with 11 other unfortunates, 5 of whom, like myself, were CW candidates. The irony of the situation was that those who had gone outside the permitted leave area to Edinburgh all got back in time. Knowing that most of those on shore leave would be there, notices were flashed on cinema screens and announcements made in dance halls and public places recalling the crew. I feared the worst. The old salts among the guards who marched us to the ship next morning fed us rumours of being strung up on the yardarm, or years in gaol, or at least dismissal from the Royal Navy with disgrace.

HMS Woolston 1st (and only) XV (Author extreme left, back row)

Woolston had in fact been out on the Methil night patrol but had returned to Rosyth the next morning, so that we were immediately summoned to the bridge. We were obviously guilty, though in extenuation we were not labelled as deserters so at least capital punishment was ruled out. We were given a hell of a bollocking by the Captain, and, then, to our relief, were weighed off with 14 days No.10As, the naval equivalent of hard labour, later reduced to 7 days. However, that was sufficient, as the punishment could only be carried out when in harbour, and enough to deny us the first and only period of home leave in prospect when the ship's boilers had to be cleaned. As we sailed that morning on our usual convoy duty, and would not be in harbour at either end until the boiler cleaning, the punishment hung over us for about two weeks.

The punishment itself seemed severe enough. We worked the seven days in harbour from 8am to 8pm on all the dirty jobs; taking gash buckets ashore, cleaning the Heads, painting ship – a foul job involving painful physical contortions working under the ship's bow – washing down the main deck with no exemption from one's turn as cook of the mess. We were mustered again after 8pm and assigned duties as Outboard Sentry which meant staying awake for another three hours each night of punishment, in my case during the Middle Watch. It seemed strange to me that we 'criminals' were entrusted with the task of looking out for possible thieves and marauders. The punishment achieved its purpose of teaching us all a lesson about obeying orders, the worst of it not being the hard work and fear of falling asleep on watch, but the loss of home leave, the breaking of a date with a very nice girl and the shame of it. Our shipmates were nothing if not sympathetic. Serving punishment was the ultimate stage to becoming a fully-fledged member of the Lower Deck.

Some days before being suddenly called aft to be told that I was to be drafted to HMS *King Alfred* to train as an officer – much to my surprise because I thought my crimes would delay matters – I took advantage of the granting of permission for relatives to visit our ship, for my home was only 30 miles away in Dundee. I told my messmates that my father was coming aboard in a few days and when they found out that he was a Professor of Zoology at the University of St. Andrews, I was on the receiving end of a good deal of chaff, for they expected him to be some sort of toff. Even my good friend Alf, kept saying that 'just because your dad's a f--------g Professor makes no difference here, and he'll just have to drink his tea out of a mug like the rest of us'. Disbelief was expressed when I said that he was a First World War veteran and knew all about being a member of the other ranks. They warned me that he might hear some filthy language but perhaps that would not matter because his ears had never been sullied with sailors' oaths and he would not understand them. He would be used to dainty teas with cucumber sandwiches and cream cakes. All this was accompanied by considerable curiosity about his occupation and whether he was absent-minded. The great day came and I met father at the gangway, showed him round the ship and entered the mess. There was a respectful silence and he was ushered to the place of honour at the head of the mess table – which had been covered with a shiny white linen tablecloth. Lashings of sandwiches were laid out and the humble best of the buns available in the NAAFI. There was a cake, I seem to recollect it being a Madeira, and we drank from cups! He got on famously with my messmates and, being a good raconteur, entertained them with stories of his soldiering days. He sang magnificently for his tea, and I felt strangely guilty at the trouble that I had caused. There was only one moment when it looked as if I was in trouble again. It had got back to the Officer of the Day that there was a Professor on board and I was soundly told off for not letting him know, so my father's departure was delayed while the officer expressed his pleasure at our being visited by someone of such eminence. My father, trying his best to suppress a smile and assuming a professorial demeanour, thanked him for conferring on his son the privilege of being a member of his crew.

If memorabilia are the measure of the grip of the past, then Margaret, my wife, and I are free of its hold. It may seem almost a sign of inverted snobbery that we do not display trophies on mantlepieces or degree certificates and other commendations on our walls and keep very few letters. But in one's 80s the present becomes in large part a digest of memories of the past and its grip tightens its hold. The writing of these memoirs is evidence enough of that. My naval memorabilia are few, but there is one particular item which I cherish from my days on the Lower Deck. During World War 2, the traditional capband with the name of your ship embroidered on it in gold thread was replaced by an inferior ribbon with only 'HMS' printed on it. There were security objections to revealing the name of your ship. A capband with a ship's name on it became a collector's item. Just before I left, one of my messmates sat down by me and said: "This'll be something to remember us by when you become a f-------g pig", and pulled out of his pocket a capband with HMS *Woolston* emblazoned on it – the real thing; and refused to take anything for it – not even rum. I have it still.

Farewell Present from the Lower Deck

Chapter 3

CHANNEL TUNNEL

———

Becoming a 'Pig'

A fortnight's leave before having to report to HMS *King Alfred* – in fact the swimming pool at Hove in peacetime – to be trained as a Cadet Rating* and to become a Temporary Acting Sub-Lieutenant RNVR offered a slight pause for breath. For months there had been no time to look ahead more than a day at a time. The name of the game had been survival with no thought for the future except the prospect of the occasional day of freedom when one might savour a night ashore and sleep in a bed with sheets. But the state of total war circumscribed any thoughts about a future outside the Navy. In any case, I had no profession to go back to and no clear aspirations which only peace might fulfil; and trying to imagine when peace would come and what opportunities it might bring was a hopeless enterprise. I had one clear ambition which was somehow to 'better my condition', to paraphrase Adam Smith, and in the course of doing so not to make too much of a fool of myself. In the short time horizon imposed on one by the war, and the full claim on my being exercised by the Royal Navy, there was only one thing to do and that was to make the best of training to become an officer and, if successful, to hope that the Lords of the Admiralty would find me employment which afforded some interest and excitement. Their Lordships lived up to expectations.

At first sight, the initiation to training as a Cadet Rating with the prospect of being awarded a commission seemed predictable. We would have to be subjected to various tests to ascertain our sanity, intelligence and motivation. We were put through the usual medical with particular interest shown in whether we had acquired any sexual diseases on the Lower Deck, and sat the conventional intelligence test. We would then face an interview with a retired naval Captain brought back into service and notorious for his bluff, irascible manner. The bush telegraph offered the information that the best way to cope with the old sea dog's impossible questions was to reply briefly and, above all, quickly. Better a wrong and confidently delivered answer than any sign of hesitation. When it came to my turn, he expressed a menacing interest in my knowledge of German and I had to swiftly disabuse him of any idea that I knew any Bavarian dialects. Then the trick question – the distance in nautical miles between Gibraltar and Malta. My rapid reply seemed to satisfy him though totally bogus. I was several hundred miles adrift. Those of us surviving this entrance examination were then paraded in full fig on the playing field of a girl's prep school outside Brighton, waiting to be addressed by the Commander who would be in charge of the first stage of our training. We were carefully inspected and imagined that we had impressed him with our turnout and enthusiasm. Then a completely bizarre and bathetic effusion greeted us. We had been brought to the pitch where, as the chosen few, we expected a stirring oration on the place of the Senior Service in the affections of the Nation, and the grave responsibilities resting on our shoulders in upholding its traditions. (We were unaware at the time of Churchill's angry comment that these traditions were a barrier to inter-service co-operation and which he listed as 'rum, sodomy and the lash'.) The Commander's bearing as he stepped up to the platform before us seemed to fit with our expectations. He had, he said, a most important announcement to make, heightening even further the drama of the occasion. As he cleared his throat, we imagined that his speech would be tied to some recent act of naval gallantry, as yet unrevealed to the public, which would inspire us to do our best. And then tumbled out his immortal words of greeting and remonstrance: "it has come to my notice that several cadet ratings have been wetting their beds…"

Becoming a Temporary Acting Sub Lieutenant (Special) RNVR was easier than I had any right to expect. I sailed through the course because I was physically fit and obviously had experience from university of taking notes for reproduction in the simple examinations designed to test what little we had to learn about seamanship, navigation and signalling. As we were drawn up to be informed who had passed and the successful ones ritually led from the parade ground to enter the wardroom I discovered, somewhat to my embarrassment, that I had been top of the class. Fortunately, there was nothing on my certificate of appointment to reveal this fact and I must appear both ungrateful and insensitive to be glad of this. The Austin Reed tailor, who had already measured me up, was relieved that he did not have to bear the risk of my failure, as he would have had to do if I had remained on the lower deck, and, transmogrified as it were, I proceeded on draft leave to home in Dundee, and in the knowledge that I would return for a revision 'Y' course in Wimbledon. The course itself was much the same as before except it included a number of WRNS who knew much more German than I did, several with university degrees and excellent company. They were the only clear indication at the time that I was destined to return to sea, for they would man the shore stations springing up along the South Coast, though this was not communicated to me. I naively assumed that this silence about my destined place was simply a security measure. The truth must have been that the Admiralty were not entirely sure how to employ commissioned 'Y' staff, for otherwise it would be difficult to explain my posting to Captain (D) Plymouth's staff in September 1943. The 'interest' and 'excitement' I sought were not the product of some great master plan in which I was designated to play some allotted role.

The young 'pig' at 22

Passing Out (author third from left, back row) August 1943

I quickly pass over the initial problems that I faced in settling down once again in a 'stone frigate'. As a rating at sea, with all the disadvantages of discomfort and demanding discipline, the ordinary things in life were predetermined – work, sleep, food, fellowship. But in Plymouth and Devonport, as a shore-based officer you had to find your own accommodation in a city continually suffering enemy air raids which reduced the supply of lodging, restaurants and cafes, and rationing brought home how well treated we had been at sea. After a brief stay in an officers' club, which had to limit stays to only a few days to allow time to look around for a more permanent abode, I eventually found lodgings where I could have bed and breakfast but no other main meals. I became a rather mysterious figure there amongst the half-dozen or so lodgers, for I occasionally disappeared for odd days, and so it became assumed that I had some hush-hush job. However, I could obtain a reasonable lunch in the Wardroom at the Devonport Barracks, and even a glass or two of sherry or whisky. I was also parted from my best girl, Margaret, who had become a WRNS officer working in London for the Ministry of Supply, adding to my gloomy existence.

Vexation fuelled my prevailing mood further, because my immediate superior, Lieutenant Hazelton, an experienced 'Headache' man, was not quite sure what to do with me. His well-meant and sage advice to me was to take it easy, enjoy the fact that I was under-employed while I could, and let events take their course – in short I was bloody lucky and had nothing to complain about. Of course, he was right, but I could not see it that way. Sending me out with some radar experts to observe how radar sets at sea were calibrated hardly increased my technical knowledge for the experts were too busy to answer my questions. We did, however, finish up in Falmouth and had a jolly time in a pub which kept rather informal opening hours. Using me to instruct some shore-based WRNS in Headache procedures was a joke, for the 'pupils' soon realised that I knew less than they did, but were very sweet and understanding. Hazelton may have known more than I realised about what was to happen to me, but did not know precisely when. It turned out to be very soon indeed.

The 'Tunnel' Disaster

It should not be difficult to appreciate that by 1943, the German naval authorities were anxious to put pressure on the Allies, and particularly island

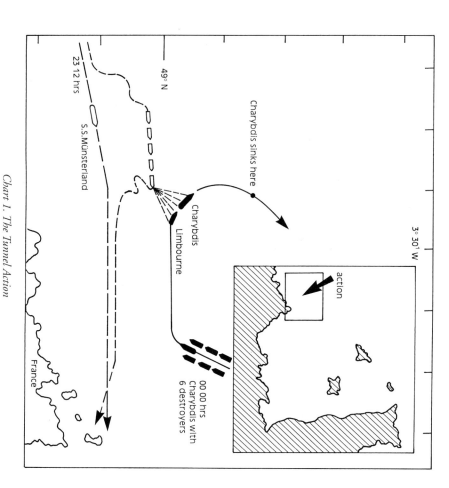

Chart 1. The Tunnel Action
(note – the dashed lines to the Charybdis and Limbourne denote torpedo tracks)

Britain, by offensive action against merchant shipping in the surrounding seas. Positioning U-boats in the Atlantic and Arctic waters was not difficult but maintaining them in operational condition and supplied with men and material required supply lines in the English Channel to be well protected. Engaging enemy forces in set piece naval battles was not considered to be a game worth the candle. If forced to engage, German destroyers in the Channel relied on firing torpedoes and a swift retreat at full speed, with gun actions avoided. Their main task was to concentrate on protection of convoys of merchant shipping supplying their bases and providing cover for their own larger surface ships, leaving E-boats to make quick sorties along the English South Coast to attack Allied shipping moving either way along the Channel.

Characteristically, the Germans followed a strict routine in facilitating the movement of seaborne traffic from Ushant on the Brittany coast to Cherbourg and onwards to the east. While this helped the collection of intelligence on the timing of movement, the strength of the escorting force and the composition of its charges, the Germans were well prepared for possible attacks. Although they had no warships larger than Elbing Class destroyers, the latter were well equipped and swifter than their British counterparts. Their flotillas were used to close co-operation and had a detailed knowledge of British naval tactics. If they lacked fire power at sea, there was compensation in the heavy guns of the coastal batteries. Their radar stations provided high quality information on movements of British shipping. And, of course, they had the tactical advantage of knowing precisely their own timetable of shipping movements. Thus by October 1943, when I was about to play my strange part in a Channel operation, it was becoming imperative to do something about the considerable amount of German shipping – including not only merchant ships but blockade runners, armed merchant raiders and naval vessels in need of refit – which was able to reach its destination safely.

It was the responsibility of Commander in Chief, Plymouth to watch for opportunities to frustrate the German intentions and the presence of a German blockade runner, *Münsterland,* in Brest together with an escort of six Elbing Class destroyers, led to a decision to conduct a sweep which would prevent the *Münsterland* reaching Cherbourg. C in C was faced with a difficult decision because the German escort was a strong one, and he had at his disposal destroyers with less firepower and less speed than the Elbings though he could muster two fleet destroyers which were of comparable strength. However, berthed at Devonport on its return from an arduous period of duty protecting Malta convoys was the light cruiser *Charybdis*, and it was decided that it should be used to cover the destroyer patrol with its senior officer in charge of the whole operation known as 'Tunnel'. Its crew, due for home leave, were hastily recalled, and several did not make it in time – they were the lucky ones. C in C must have known that there were considerable risks involved in this decision. As well as the relatively low speed of the Hunt destroyers and their fewer torpedo tubes, there was no time for tactical training, all the more necessary when the command ship had no experience of this type of operation. Furthermore, the newly appointed captain of *Limbourne*, Commander Phipps – who by coincidence had been the captain of *Woolston* when I first joined her – had barely time to introduce himself to his officers and, through no fault of his own, was late for C in C's briefing meeting. As the captain of the leading Hunt Class destroyer, the others being *Talybont*, *Wensleydale* and *Stevenstone* (which had to be borrowed from C in C Portsmouth), his role was crucial. So far as my personal history is concerned, what turned out to be particularly important was that *Charybdis* was neither equipped with Headache nor had its captain any experience of its role in naval operations. Had that been so, I suppose that I would have found myself as a temporary member of his crew, but instead I was rushed 'on special duty' to the *Limbourne* so joining my old skipper, who remembered me, seemed pleased to have Headache at his disposal, but clearly not knowing much more than I did what sort of operation we would be engaged in.

Very full accounts from British and German official records exist, covering the disaster of operation Tunnel together with eye-witness accounts. I offer a digest of these in order to highlight the contrast between what is now known about what happened compared with the unfolding of events as I viewed them at the time.

Following C in C Plymouth's instructions, the cruiser and six destroyers left Plymouth on 22 October at 1900 hours in single line* ahead and proceeded SE at a speed of 17 knots to arrive at 0030 hours at a position about 30 miles west of Jersey. As planned, the force then turned westward and reduced speed to 13 knots in the expectation that the cruiser and fleet destroyers could engage the enemy escort, perhaps an hour and a half after this alteration of course, while the Hunt Class destroyers would be detached to attack the convoy which would now be vulnerable after the loss of protection.

The plan assumed that radio silence, restricted radar transmission, and Asdic silence would minimize enemy detection of the force's movement. Whether the absence of the mention of a specific target, the *Münsterland*, and of the composition of the enemy escort in the plan was a security measure is not known though this has been interpreted as evidence that none of the British captains knew what was to be the specific target and the strength of opposition. If that interpretation is correct, it explains some of the extraordinary confusion that followed. But the assumption that enemy detection would be avoided up to the moment of visual contact was in any case a false one.

The subsequent manoeuvres that brought the opposing forces into contact are somewhat complicated to describe, but the essence of what happened is shown in the accompanying map. The situation would have been almost comical if tragedy had not resulted. The Germans already had information of our presence from shore radar but were not aware of the precise size and composition of our force. What was important was that the Germans were already tracking our westerly course of 267 degrees and were simply waiting for us to come into a position where they could launch a torpedo attack. We had spasmodic indications of their presence well before 0100. Just after 0100 I picked up some unintelligible speech, which denoted that the enemy was very close, probably representing at least three destroyers. This information was passed by our Captain to *Charybdis* but its Captain and staff interpreted 'Y' information as 'my' information which did not indicate the technical authority of the message, which was ignored. About half an hour later I was able to identify six call signs and a clear indication of a command structure denoting preparations for an attack, but we had no idea of the position of the enemy craft. I thought that my training was fully justified when I reported that the German craft had an order to fire immediately 18 torpedoes, which I excitedly reported to Commander Phipps, but it was only a few minutes later that there was a colossal explosion, I was carried upward so that my head hit the bulkhead and my fellow operator was lying on the deck and groaning with pain. Then there was complete silence.

I had often wondered how I would face up to battle conditions and like my shipmates tried hard to suppress any fears of mortal danger; having to concentrate on tracking the enemy was enough to take one's mind off any cowardly thoughts – after all on board a ship one can hardly run away! My first reaction to the explosion was one of intense relief. I was alive and apparently only suffering from a bang on the head and a gash on the leg. I found myself acting in a decisive, almost mechanical, way. If we stayed afloat then it might be useful to remain on watch, but the explosion had rendered our equipment out of action. I should therefore find out if I could be of use elsewhere which meant reporting to the bridge. I struggled up the port gangway, learning in the process that we had a heavy list to starboard, making first to the wheelhouse and then to the bridge. In the dark I could only discern a few figures who seemed to be like waxworks, immovable and totally silent, but for some intermittent and disturbing groans. I recognized nobody, which was not surprising as I had joined *Limbourne* only hours before. From the bridge I looked ahead and then began to realise the extent of the damage – the bows had been blown off and we must be shipping water. I went below to see what I could do for my much more severely wounded 'oppo' but there were much worse cases being succoured by those who had been as lucky as myself, and I could only assure him that he would not be forgotten if we had to abandon ship. I then had the disturbing thought that, being so close to the French coast, *Limbourne* would finish up as a beached wreck and be thoroughly searched by the Germans. So I returned to the Headache cabin, lugged our S27 receiver out on deck and with great difficulty, because of its bulk and weight, threw it overboard. I returned to the cabin realising that the Code Book of German signals should be destroyed, but by now the cabin was under two feet of water and I could not find it. (As I discovered many years later, the existence of Headache was well known to the Germans.) Eventually – actually probably only half an hour or so later – I made for the after deck where survivors were beginning to congregate, and where the Coxswain was making frantic efforts to bring the auxiliary steering into use. Having taken the wheel on *Woolston* under the supervision of the Quartermaster* I naively offered to help him, but he restrained himself from saying what he thought of my idea. Surprisingly, *Limbourne* managed to get steam up, but attempts to get under way, if possible to get clear of the French coast, were proved to be futile for the response to the steering system was for the ship to go round in circles. Clearly it was necessary to look for help and it was in the process of doing so that we found out that what we thought was our nearest support, the *Charybdis*, had not only been hit but was sinking fast, and was to suffer massive casualties. Contact with the remaining force, now under *Grenville's* command, could not be made, not knowing that its captain made the reasonable assumption that we must have been attacked by E-boats which could be expected to congregate round the wrecks waiting to do battle with any ships looking for survivors. So apparently left to our fate, orders were given by the young Sub-Lieutenant Cunliffe-Owen, now in command, to prepare to abandon ship. That would have been a difficult enough operation if we were to look after the many wounded in the explosion, but then, after what appeared to be an age, our Yeoman of Signals made contact with *Talybont* which had been detached to find survivors, leaving the other ships to sweep westwards in search of enemy craft. By the time they returned to our position at about 0500 hours, *Talybont* had conducted a model rescue operation under very difficult weather conditions. In the case of walking wounded like myself, this entailed watching for the moment when the decks of *Limbourne* and *Talybont* were aligned and then jumping from the former to the latter, doing my damaged leg no good, but immensely relieved to find I was back if not on dry land at least on solid steel. I remember little about the next few hours before we reached Plymouth Sound fifteen hours after we had left it. I horrified the Headache operator on *Talybont* by my bloody and unkempt appearance coupled with an enormous black eye and must have been expertly bandaged up before we tied up at Devonport. I was certainly unaware that *Talybont* had endeavoured to take *Limbourne* in tow and that when this failed it had taken until near daylight to have her sunk by torpedo. Small consolation after such a disaster that neither *Limbourne* nor its survivors would now not fall into German hands. So 30 officers and 432 ratings from *Charybdis* and about one hundred crew of *Limbourne* were not to return home.

Aftermath

I suppose that nowadays (2003) we survivors would have been subjected to some form of counselling to mitigate the shock of disaster. The Navy had set procedures of a different kind for this situation; check on the condition of the survivors and hospitalise those who needed immediate medical attention; follow up by the issue of Wound and Hurt certificates signed by a naval surgeon to produce the necessary evidence if a later claim were made for a War Pension; convene immediately a Court of Inquiry and hold on to those who would be called to give evidence while their memories of what happened were sharp and clear; then issue travel warrants and passes for two weeks survivors' leave; then recall to duty.

I have nothing but admiration for the speed with which I was treated skilfully and rapidly for my head wound and my Wound and Hurt certificate was issued only two days after reaching Devonport. I refused hospitalisation, accepting a generous offer by Hazleton and his wife to stay with them until I could make for home. I did have trouble sleeping but it was weeks later before I suffered what may have been after effects and this took the embarrassing form of 'the runs'. My 'oppo' was not so fortunate, but cheerful enough and thankful to have been rescued. Whatever the disadvantages of only a few hours contact with *Limbourne* crew, we were both saved grieving for lost friends. The only emotional experience associated with the crew came later when I went home to Dundee and had to describe what had happened to *Limbourne* to the father of one of its stokers who had been killed in the explosion. Meeting in the November gloom in one of the poorest districts of the town the injustice of fate seemed all the more apparent – why his son and not me?

In plain language – A bang on the head and an enormous black eye!

I remember the Court of Inquiry held only a day or two after the sinkings, less for my own attempts to answer its questions and more for an interesting insight into the motivation of the surviving career Royal Navy officers. First the interrogation. It was clear that the Court had only a general idea of the operation of Headache and little appreciation of the element of uncertainty in being able to pick up, transcribe and interpret R/T signals rapidly delivered. My evidence for this lies not only in the questions asked and my answers as to the information I had passed up to Commander Phipps but what must have been a subsequent release of information to those who have written about Operation Tunnel. There it is suggested, as in Smith's admirable Chapter on 'Tunnel' in *Hold the Narrow Seas*, that *Charybdis* was handicapped by the 'inadequate' Headache reports from his 'consorts'. (I have been informed by the Naval Historical Branch that they cannot trace any reference to a transcription of the Court of Inquiry's findings.) It was an incident during the foregathering of officers before being called to give evidence that intrigued me. Four regular officers, who were not wounded or were walking wounded, drew aside from the 'temps' like myself and agreed to co-ordinate their accounts of the action with the clear intention of increasing their chances of receiving some form of commendation, possibly leading to a Mention in Dispatches. I have no reason to suppose that those concerned behaved other than as they would be expected to do in a disastrous naval operation, but the incident brought home to me that those who were career officers had a different future to consider than those of us who merely wished to survive and return to Civvy Street.*

So to survivors' leave and a wonderful reception from Margaret and her family. No one in her family or mine seemed to be surprised when we announced our engagement. We married the following February, one acquaintance giving our union six months, but it seemed somehow to have lasted, having passed the Golden Wedding mark in 1994.

The final stage in the set procedure of rehabilitation was to report back to Plymouth for duty. Hazleton predicted that I was bound to spend the rest of my naval career in a 'stone frigate' as a 'reward' for my experiences. I duly reported to Captain (D) Plymouth, a gruff but fatherly old (probably 50ish!) salt who, after congratulating me on my engagement, gave me my orders to report to DSD (9) Admiralty who controlled Headache postings. Was I returning to suburbia Wimbledon once again, only round the corner from Margaret's home and possibly appointed to its staff? I could not see that happening. I reported to DSD (9) and was questioned once again about my experiences. I neither expected nor received any commiseration but was astonished to be admonished for consigning the S27 to the vasty deep – "very valuable and expensive equipment, Peacock", according to the Lieutenant Commander sitting in his comfortable office off the Mall. What was I supposed to do, when it was already unserviceable – lug it back to Whitehall? I had learnt enough not to protest at this kind of inane suggestion. There was in any case a change of duties already arranged for me that concentrated my mind wonderfully, and why will soon be apparent.

Sailors' Splicing February 1944

There was a personal sequel many years later. When I became Principal of the independent University College (later University) of Buckingham, one of its Council members, Peter (later Sir Peter) Crill, invited me in 1981 to Jersey for a fund raising expedition. Meeting me at the airport, he enquired if this was my first visit and I told him how once I had been rather close to calling under rather unusual circumstances. As a boy, Peter had witnessed the burial service at Mont-a-l'Abbe Cemetery of the last of 29 bodies of the crews washed ashore in Jersey. Although a muted occasion, the Germans did provide a firing party and guard of honour and allowed official wreaths to be laid on the coffins. These and other bodies washed ashore were subsequently re-interred in a special Island War Cemetery. The Germans severely censored all references to these ceremonies in local publications, being rather jumpy about a repeat of a similar but more prominent event already held in Guernsey where 5000 islanders had turned up to what became a civil but orderly demonstration of loyalty. Although it was November, nine hundred floral wreaths were laid on the graves. Not surprisingly, they banned civilian attendance at subsequent burials of British servicemen. Peter took me to the Island War Cemetery and left me there to my thoughts.

This bitter experience confirms that the pre-conditions for the successful use of Y information were not in place, as least at command level. The information was obtained and passed as speedily as possible to those who could use it. It must be an open question whether other enemy signals of significance could have been missed in our scan, but this seems doubtful. Comparing notes with the experienced operator on *Talybont*, the next Hunt destroyer in line, indicated that we had recorded and reported the same information. The important pre-condition that command should be aware of the contribution of Y information and how to use it was missing. Again, it could be argued that the disaster could not have been avoided on the basis of use of that information alone, but there is one piece of evidence that favours the opposite argument. The captain of *Talybont* used the Y information to reduce the risk of being hit by making a quick alteration of course to face the direction of the attack and successfully avoided being 'fished'. There were other lessons learned from the 'Tunnel' disaster, such as the importance of air support for operations of this kind, but I am not competent to discuss these.

I cannot prove that the Tunnel disaster had any bearing on the subsequent organization of Y services in similar situations. What is well-documented is that they were extensively employed by the Royal Navy in their support of the Allied invasion of Normandy in 1944.

Chapter 4

THE SHARP END OF THE CODE BUSINESS

Using Enigma at Sea

Reminiscences of WW2 are legion for the Royal Navy ranging from Monserrat's famous *The Cruel Sea* with the intermingling of personal and professional drama, to the highly entertaining *Not Entitled* of the now famous English don Frank Kermode with its hilarious account of the 'mad captains' who controlled his wartime destiny as a junior officer in the secretarial branch. The gradual revelations which release of public documents has produced regarding the role played by the cipher and code breakers has perhaps kept alive some interest in their crucial role in affecting the course of the war; and when this is shown to link up with the contribution of mathematics to the development of the computer, and with the particular fortunes of Alan Turing, the events of over half a century ago maintain an interest which might otherwise have vanished well before the Millenium.

Whether that interest extends from the romance and drama of the Enigma story to the activities of those who had to apply code breaking to particular war-time operations is for the reader to judge. The story itself contains graphic accounts of how such operations at sea and on land relied on the revelations of enemy intentions in their decoded messages but there is only a handful of accounts of the building up of a managerial system which enabled intelligence derived from such sources to be brought into play in decisions to frustrate enemy intentions. Aileen Clayton's *The Enemy is Listening: The Story of the Y Service (1980)* is one such account which is particularly valuable as a personal record of the 'Y' origins within the RAF. Her analysis of the less glamorous but absorbing details of processing and using intelligence information has encouraged me to believe that my own assignment adds something to the story. One has also to remember the part played by the Royal Navy itself in capturing apparatus and documents from German U-boats and surface ships which assisted Bletchley in keeping up-to-date with cipher and coding changes. Apart from the dangers involved in attacking and boarding craft in order to obtain such items, there was one aspect of their success in doing so which was to prove of importance in my own involvement in monitoring German radio messages. This was to leave the Germans in the dark, so far as was possible, about the extent of the capture of such valuable spoils. It entailed warning those engaged in capture about the high security rating of what they were doing, in interrogation of prisoners and censoring their mail and decoding any W/T messages sent by the German warships before capture which might indicate how far crews had been able to conceal or destroy apparatus or information.

The Navy's interest in using German communications to their Forces was not confined to the procedures of the Kriegsmarine. Certainly, engagements with German warships, including both surface craft and U-boats, might be more successfully conducted if one could anticipate their movements as revealed by communication with each other and with shore bases and the Kriegsmarine High Command. However, of cardinal importance, particularly in the Arctic, was advance knowledge of German aircraft movements. German torpedo bombers based on Norwegian airfields had been a force to be reckoned with in trying to protect convoys to Russia. German weather planes flying from such fields, although unarmed, covered vast distances of the Arctic as far over as Greenland and could transmit sightings of Allied warship and merchant ship movements. Of less immediate importance was German ship-to-shore communication which involved the Wehrmacht. The grim fate of the earlier convoys to Russia, notably the famous PQ17, all too clearly indicated that those in charge of convoy protection and strikes against German shipping would need immediate access to what was known by Bletchley not only about German naval but also air and surface communication in their area of operation. This meant having to solve a number of problems. We now know a great deal about the marvellous ingenuity employed in Bletchley to scan German intelligence sources but, as already explained in Chapter 1, there was a technical difficulty of communication with naval forces more than a thousand miles away where messages might not get through because of 'skip' distances which disrupted W/T signals. A partial solution lay in attaching naval intelligence personnel to the staff of the commander of particular operations. These officers would need to be trained to decode German signals, sometimes requiring them to try their hand at deciphering them before Bletchley could supply the code used by the Germans on any particular day. They would need to supervise W/T ratings with a special aptitude for reading German W/T signals. Specialist skills of this kind hardly existed in the Royal Navy and trained staff would have to be placed in a position where they were immediately on call. However, this meant being attached to the Home Fleet at Scapa Flow whereas the training and briefing facilities which could only be made available by the RAF were concentrated in Cheadle, Staffordshire. Initially, the RAF supplied commissioned and non-commissioned officers to the Home Fleet who supervised naval W/T ratings, but, apart from the administrative complications that this produced, the RAF were not likely to continue this arrangement, given the pressure on their resources with the growing prospect of bringing the war to Europe.

From R/T to W/T

Solving these problems must have been a matter of some urgency. Immediately after survivor's leave the Admiralty directed my steps South South West from the Citadel (which still juts out into the Mall in London) to an address in Horseferry Road. I was ushered into a room where the occupant was sitting behind a huge desk with his back to me. He swung round suddenly, blinked and smiled and handed me a passage in German to translate on the spot. I did not find it too difficult and before I had finished it he grunted, nodded approvingly and we had a congenial conversation which I seem to remember explored a joint interest in music. In retrospect I realised that he had learnt a good deal about me without trying very hard and without any suggestion that he was conducting an interrogation. A day or so after that pleasant afternoon, the serious purpose of the interview was revealed. I was now to be trained in the interpretation of German W/T signalling and assigned with four other junior officers to intelligence work covering operations in the Arctic carried out under the command of C in C Home Fleet based at Scapa Flow. Oh yes – my 'interrogator' . His name meant nothing to me at the time, but it was

'Josh' Cooper, much later to be revealed as one of the key figures in the Bletchley teams that received the highest commendation of Churchill. I spare the reader the details of the intensive training which was undertaken in a country house north of Rugby – now overshadowed by the M6 Motorway. My most vivid memories of it are a totally incomprehensible lecture by a lady mathematician from Bletchley who appeared to suffer from the itch, and making several dashes to London to see Margaret, arriving back at Rugby station in the middle of the night and then riding a rickety bicycle without lights back to camp, hopefully in time to catch three hours' sleep before being back in the classroom.

It is easy to imagine, as I did, that the next stage would be placement on HMS *Rodney* attached to the C-in-C Home Fleet's staff swinging round a buoy in Scapa Flow and awaiting assignment to one or other fighting patrols or escort forces where eavesdropping on the enemy might assist naval strategy or tactics. One would then disappear on some operation or other and, subject to survival which seemed more likely now (1944) than in 1941, would return to report to my immediate superior. At all events, one would be a member of a team forming professional and social relationships which would be moral support for a youngster of 21. This exercise in imagination was tempered with the expectation that something of this kind was the only rational outcome, but I could not have guessed at what was to follow for the five officers – four of us W/T intelligence specialists and one 'Headache' officer – who were lined up to add this rather new dimension to Naval intelligence in Northern Waters.

Serving Four Masters

The four W/T officers and their rating operators had to be assigned to a 'ship' somewhere and we found ourselves based in HMS *Proserpine*, not some splendidly named cruiser swinging round the next buoy to *Rodney* in Scapa Flow but a set of Nissen Huts on the Island of Hoy. Our confrères, mostly engaged in responsible jobs keeping the Home Fleet operational, were very tolerant of our presence although we were an odd bunch, all newly commissioned and therefore with no seniority and yet puzzlingly engaged on work of high security. The clue to their acceptance of us lay in their recognition that we all had done sea time and three of us had been in awkward engagements with the enemy, and I suppose were not quite as barmy as they might have been led to expect.

Our relationship with the top brass in this stone frigate was less secure because we could not be ordered to perform the routine duties and subscribe to the rituals of life in a naval base. On one famous occasion to be recorded later, this led to a remarkable clash with one of us. One long term repercussion of this formal attachment to a shore establishment was that some of our telegraphists who were to spend many months at sea were later to be refused the Atlantic Star medal because there was no record that they had ever been afloat. In one particular case, even fifty years after the event, I found myself arguing with the Ministry of Defence about the injustice of denying the medal to one member of our team and, but for the intervention of his local MP, William Cash, it would not have been rectified.

Of course, our orders to proceed on particular operations, of the kind I shall later describe, came from C-in-C Home Fleet, conveyed to us, I seem to remember, through the Staff Officer Intelligence (SOI) of *Proserpine*. Although we could discern from the orders that they originated with the SOI Home Fleet, it was some time before any of us was able to identify this second source of immediate authority over our service lives. His reputation preceded contact made with us directly and indicated a super-intelligence, an officer holding in his grasp closely-guarded secrets of immense importance and a high degree of cultural sensitivity illustrated by an awesome habit of turning in at night by reading a full orchestral score. (This last piece of information particularly intrigued us as we all played a musical instrument.) Again, like Josh Cooper, it was only years later that one realised that he had an important if elusive role in the Enigma story which culminated in his appointment as Admiral Sir Bruce Fraser's adviser during the *Scharnhorst* battle which had taken place very shortly before our arrival at Scapa. When eventually we were in touch with him, it was by ship-shore telephone during which he spoke in a stage whisper. In the course of eighteen months during which I went on fifteen separate operations in Arctic waters, I met Lieutenant Commander Edward Thomas RNVR in person only once. Although he could be charming on the telephone and tried hard to convey the impression that we were colleagues engaged in exacting high-grade intelligence work, and not simply junior staff there to do his bidding, he always left it to the last moment to change plans in such a way as to maximize adverse reactions to his, normally bad, news. We must all have experienced at some time a recall to be ready for some sudden emergency, and while this might be disappointing if it meant cancellation of leave, it would not have been resented if ultimately one had not found that it was often a false alarm. This fissiparous relationship could not have been entirely his fault. The alarm bells were not sounded by him but by his superiors faced with sudden calls for action – which might later be cancelled – and he would not want to take chances. We clearly did not fully appreciate his position and security considerations may have prevented him from putting us enough in the picture so that we would obey his orders without rancour and complaint. However, I am bound to say, that, while not sure that I would have known how to handle our awkward squad and young Peacock in particular, man management did not appear to be his strong point. As I hope to show, the jobs did get done in the end and some of us got more recognition than we deserved. The rationale of basing us ashore was clear enough for we could then be more easily assigned to any one of a number of ships which carried an Admiral's pennant. Obligations to two masters might be a minor inconvenience. However, our position was much more complicated than this, for moving up the learning curve quickly and remaining proficient depended on close contact with those who were monitoring the continuing change in enemy communications. This was particularly true of the activities of the German Air Force operating in Norway, reconnoitring and attacking Allied shipping and their escorts. The long-established centre which was to fuel our efforts was based several hundred miles from Scapa in RAF Cheadle, Staffs. In fact, after initial briefing near Rugby, we spent several weeks getting to grips with the technique of turning to practical account the information on enemy communications supplied by the Bletchley super-boffins.

So now we would have to contend with a third administrative hierarchy headed by a Wing Commander Swanborough. We must have created some headaches for him as an extra responsibility, but he and his staff could not have been more helpful. They adopted the time-honoured British principle used in the textile mills of 'sitting with Nellie', by which we watched an experienced RAF intelligence officer de-coding actual messages and in the course of time putting together the information in order to demonstrate what we could find out about enemy movements. A few of these officers had actually been on naval operations and this added even more credibility to their method of instruction. I hold only one grudge against RAF Cheadle which was their insistence that, in a War Weapons Week* parade, I should train and command a contingent of our W/T ratings to march through the streets of Cheadle and salute some bigwig on a platform. As the Senior Service we had to lead the parade. It is as well that there was no senior Royal Navy presence on that occasion for we would have been charged with bringing the Royal Navy into disrepute by our ignorance of naval drill and slovenly appearance. I have a suspicion that the

Wing Commander knew what would happen and the RAF contingent would put us to shame!

The temptation to examine the integration of a migrant population of sailors with their RAF counterparts and the local Staffordshire population must be avoided though it would make a rather fascinating story. The ratings settled in, in some cases very comfortably, rather better than their officers, and some actually remained at Cheadle after WW2 and married local girls. I must concentrate on the managerial problems of conducting business with four separate 'bosses', including the Admiralty, although our connection with the last-named became somewhat remote until the war in Europe ended. They were kept in touch by copies of our 'Secret' reports on each operation and only occasionally raised some query about our doings.

The major problem was that when any doubt arose about where we should be located, readiness for any operation implied that we should have up-to-date briefing. This meant a pendulum-like logistical movement between Scapa and Cheadle and intimate acquaintance with the notorious 'Jellicoe', the daily train which traversed the UK from London to Thurso. It left Euston at 10.00am and our party of two officers – on some occasions one officer and a RAF Intelligence Sergeant – and a dozen or so ratings were first of all transported to Stoke-on-Trent railway station and then took the slow train to Crewe to join it.

There were several problems to be faced which could never be satisfactorily solved. Two of these are obvious – finding somewhere to sit on a train, invariably late, and which was likely to be full already and likely to remain so for close on 24 hours, and the wearisome nature of the journey itself, staggering up the Shap with engines pulling in front and pushing from behind, stopping in Perth to change crews and engines, and finally arriving at Thurso the following morning, in winter being greeted by howling gales and snowstorms. It must be admitted that at Thurso it was possible to have an excellent breakfast at one of two small hotels where war-time rationing did not seem to have penetrated. But then the real test of one's sea legs was to be faced – the screw motion of the famous old tub that conveyed us over the treacherous Pentland Firth. Many are the breakfasts that did not follow a more natural process during that journey. It was almost a symbol of sadism that the tub provided as good a lunch as the Thurso hotel breakfasts with second helpings when the clientele was confined to the intrepid few. I date my completion of a rite of passage as a sailor from the day I was able to go below decks to the dining room during a particularly rough crossing.

The unexpected problem was the 'murder bag', so christened because it contained an amount of coding documents which weighed approaching 40 lbs. It seemed to be a modified mailbag with a special lock and key and a chain. The officer in charge of the team had strict instructions not to let it out of his sight and preferably to attach the chain to his wrist. In theory, this valuable impediment to movement could entitle one to demand a separate carriage in a train because of the security risk of loss or theft, but it would have been laughable to have attempted to persuade the transport officer at Crewe that this entitlement should be enforced. Only on one occasion did I manage successfully to demand a separate carriage but I was well prepared with a document which supported this entitlement. A very puzzled transport officer, even younger than myself, reluctantly authorised me to travel in such style from Inverness to Perth. As soon as we were clear of Inverness, I filled the carriage with members of the PBI (poor bloody infantry) who might have had to stand all the way – my self-satisfaction at this act of generosity was sickening in the extreme.

But now conveyed to Scapa and transferred by a commandeered trawler to Lyness and so to *Proserpine* and tired out after the long land journey, one hoped that the impending operation where our skills would be tested might be delayed long enough to get a good night's sleep – unless, that is, one fell in with some hospitable company who insisted that the only cure to a return to the dark days of an Orkney winter was an extended bibulous evening.

To complete this introduction to the managerial aspects of Y service, I must list the other 'subs' who were members of this travelling circus. Allan Jay was a cashier in an insurance company, good pianist, fervent Catholic, already having experienced being sunk on HMS *Berkeley* in the Dieppe Raid. Jack Horder had been a teller in a bank and he had been aboard HMS *Edinburgh* when it was torpedoed in the Barents Sea. Victor Kanter, South African recently down from Oxford where he had been a contemporary of Denis Healey, who had just become commissioned in the South African Navy. Jack Davies was the Headache Officer, like Kanter and Jay interested in music, and in Civvy Street a tax inspector. And then myself, younger than all of them and without occupation who by the accident of service bureaucracy happened to be senior to them all; and this had, as I shall show, some curious results.

Chapter 5

THE CHRONOLOGY OF EAVESDROPPING

——

Preparation

So now HMS *Proserpine* is reached and some assignment awaited. The W/T ratings are settling in their own quarters under the watchful eye of Chief Petty Officer Marsland who knows how to identify the *juste milieu* between keeping their W/T speeds up to the mark and making sure that they are let off the disciplinary hook in order to enjoy some of the rather restricted delights of this isolated shore base. He is well aware that they are going to work hard under far from comfortable conditions when they go aboard whatever ship carries the flag for a coastal raid, a Russian convoy or some such operation. He is also an expert advice-giver to junior officers whom he knows are wettish behind the ears but does not despise them as mere Hostilities Only, Saturday Night Sailors. They may have been ratings, too, but, while he is glad that they have had that experience and some of them have seen action, they are now to be tested by the confidence they engender in those who work for them. He has a pen picture in his mind for every rating and conveys what his officer charges need to know about them but with fairness and discretion. He is equally adept at knowing when his officers need advice and some nicely-put admonition. He has also trained up a small number of Leading Telegraphists, HOs like ourselves, notably Leading Telegraphist Skipworth who does him great credit by growing into a splendid deputy. When doubts may have arisen in my mind about the value of the traditions of the Royal Navy, I think of those regulars such as CPO Marsland and am obliged to dismiss these doubts from my mind.

A signal arrives and our usual contingent of two officers, one Leading Telegraphist and 12 ratings are mustered for our next operation. The signal simply contains the name of the ship and nothing about the operation itself but in time we gain enough experience to know that if it is an aircraft or escort carrier there is a high probability that this means North Russia on convoy escort duty; if a cruiser or battleship, more likely to be a further raid to try to sink the *Tirpitz* still afloat in Tromso Fjord or on coastal convoys moving along the Norwegian coast. The only curious exception for Victor Kanter and myself was to muster at Greenock just after D-Day along with Norwegian troops, all of us about to board a cruiser, but, as recounted later, our guess about our destination was badly out. The type of vessel makes little difference either to the procedures to be followed for our duties or to the duties themselves.

The Eavesdroppers

All Aboard

The lighter takes the contingent alongside the waiting ship, already in a state of preparedness, and the gangway party groan as it arrives. It is the signal for departure, the harbingers of trouble ahead for it only turns up when action is expected, and the messdeck rumours that the ship may be due for a refit down South (with leave prospects!) are unfounded. The unspoken, colourful naval curses are written all over their faces. Quarters are assigned and the necessary enquiries are made about working space and our own accommodation.

The usual regrets are offered about working space. This depends on the luck of the draw. It had to be capable of allowing good reception and usually that meant being above decks. In eighteen months Victor and I found ourselves having to keep ratings happy in anything from a large locker used for stowing unused gear to placement below the after gun turret. With no rank to pull, accommodation depended on the good offices of senior ship and flag staff and therefore their views on how useful we might be. One means of redress which could be employed retrospectively, was an official report at the end of the operations which went to an impressive variety of bigwigs from C in C Home Fleet, the Flag Officer in charge of the operation and the ship's captain to the intelligence chiefs at the Admiralty.

On one sortie – in which I did not take part – Victor was sent on his own on a hurriedly prepared operation off the Norwegian Coast. I learnt a great deal from him about how to draft official reports, and could not have matched his splendid tongue-in-cheek observation in his official report on this experience that 'accommodation consisted of a vacant space in a disused passage which was half the size of the Admiral's bathroom'. This caused him to be summoned by the captain, rather rattled by this piece of *chutzpah* and Victor bluffed it out by claiming that such comparisons were only designed to give an objective impression of the difficulties faced by both ourselves and the ship in solving the problem of coping with supernumerary personnel. Captain Denny, after complimenting Victor on the useful contribution made to the operation, grinned and said: "Next time, you can hae the Admiral's bathroom".

Usually, officers were simply assigned whatever surplus accommodation was available. Perhaps one of their officers was on leave or assigned elsewhere or more likely as juniors we would be found a bunk somewhere because the wartime complement of the ship was much greater than expected. We would be members of the Wardroom for the duration of the operation – but there was one unexpected exception. Battleships were much more correct than other craft and precedent did not allow officers under the age of 23 to be members of the Wardroom. They would be assigned to the Gun Room along with the Midshipmen. When Victor and I arrived on board HMS *Anson*, we created a precedential crisis, for he was over 23 and I was under 23, but I was his senior officer and in charge of the party! I have already indicated Victor's diplomatic skills and he announced that he would be very happy to forgo his rights and join me in the Gun Room. I suspect he already knew that this not only created goodwill, but meant that our seniority in the Gun Room would entail being treated with much respect, care and attention. He was right.

Procedure

What is now described is a digest of the activities common to most of the operations on which our contingents were engaged. We become temporary members of the staff of the senior officer in charge of the operation, usually a Vice Admiral but immediately responsible to his Staff Officer of Operations (SOO), usually a regular three-ringer Commander, and report to the Admiral only through him. The Admiral will hoist his pennant on the senior ship, at least a cruiser with a four-ring Captain and to whom I am responsible for good order and naval discipline of my team. The Captain may not be familiar with our role, and mildly worried about having 'boffins' on board who scarcely know what a marlin-spike looks like; but he will usually thaw out and can be a useful ally. We were not there to impress him, but on at least one occasion Victor and I were useful in being able to communicate with Russian officers who came aboard when our convoys reached the Kola Inlet on their way to Murmansk. If English was unknown to them we could try out our French and German. (The Captain would remember the stories about the stripping of the cabin fittings of HMS *Belfast* by Russian officers on one such visit so that the possibility of a knowledge of their language might act as a deterrent if there were an attempt at a further act of larceny, though in our experience this never took place. Victor and I were once complimented on our communication skills when Russian officers claimed to know no English, believing that we spoke to them in their native tongue. We kept quiet about the fact that we used the language of our common enemy.)

Once installed in whatever improvised accommodation had been found for receiving sets and a space, other than on our knees, for decoding books and notes, the W/T operators are divided into three 'watches' of four ratings covering

24 hours. Allowance has to be made for the intensity of being constantly on the alert so that those on watch can have brief intervals of rest, though remaining on the job, but there must always be two sets at any one time scanning the airwaves. The watch routine will also depend upon the incidence and type of radio traffic. They have to be particularly alert in the early morning when the German weather planes begin their hazardous journey north of the Arctic Circle, starting with tuning signals and then regular reporting of their position and weather reports at regular intervals during the morning and sometimes well into the afternoon. Any unusual events, such as sightings of shipping, would also be transmitted, and two-way transmission ensures that the weather planes are being kept informed about changes in plans which might affect them, such as the landing conditions at their home airfield. Additionally, coverage extends to land-sea contact with U-boats which itself might be generated by sightings of Allied shipping reported by the weather planes. Sometimes, too, lookout is kept for ship-to-shore traffic along the Norwegian coast, particularly if our operations entail supporting attacks on coastal shipping movements.

Operators become very skilled at recognizing the style of keying by particular German operators – air or shore-based. 'Fritz' sending shore-to-air signals might key at a much faster rate than 'Hans' who might work at a slower and perhaps variable speed. If a weather plane sends out a message, it will begin with a call sign identifying the aircraft and its base, followed by a time of dispatch and then a message giving the position of the aircraft and a weather report. The message is sent out in groups of three letters, each group representing a number of possibilities. These might be individual letters with a number of groups making up a word; some groups can be shorthand ways of expressing map references in longitude and latitude; and there might be groups which represent low level coding of message material such as a sighting of ships or other aircraft which cuts down on transmission time.

In an ideal world, once a W/T operator hands us such a message, we should be able to decode it by information received about the code of the day as identified by Bletchley and sent to the Flag Officer in charge. Information on the position of the aircraft, its weather report and perhaps some further information of interest to the aircraft's base might then be obtained. Even this takes time and only experience reduces the time taken.

However, there are often difficulties in having 'clean copy' of the kind described. First, radio interference can make it difficult for the operator to provide clean copy, so that in this case we might have to deduce what the missing or corrupted coded groups might contain. Secondly, full information may not be available to be able to decode the shorthand used, so that again the meaning of the relevant groups has to be deduced. The real challenge, however, comes from the situation where the necessary information from Bletchley which enables us to look up the correct pages of code books for the code of the day is not received. This situation is most likely to occur in the very early morning when the code change is already in force. However quickly Bletchley is able to identify the code used, there is still the problem of getting the information speedily to users. As already explained there are technical problems encountered which made delay a regular occurrence. This only matters if W/T traffic starts very early in the day. During the severe winter weather in the Arctic, even the intrepid weather planes might be delayed or flights cancelled, depending not only on the weather conditions during flight but also at take-off at their base. Faced with these problems the urgency of their solution depends on whether the operation might be affected in any way by enemy reporting. This is a rare occurrence but one is not likely to know this until after the event.

With only the coded message before us there are various ways to analyse it. W/T operators might recognize who was in contact with the weather planes by their 'visiting card' – their style and speed of transmission. This might reveal the home base of the plane. Knowing something of the flight path of planes from that base and the likely time of take-off, some idea of its position can be obtained. The length of the message sent to base by the plane will vary according to the information to be reported. Ordinary weather reports will be transmitted in messages of fairly standard length, but if something unusual happens, the messages are longer. With some idea of the position of the plane and length of message the Staff Officer (Operations) might have other information which might offer a clue to whether or not the plane had spotted something of interest.

The Musical Enemy

Cracking the code for the day is beyond our resources, but a curious feature of ground-air transmission makes it just worth having a go. There was one German telegraphist – based I seem to remember at Bodø – who sent out tuning signals of varying length at regular intervals, and it was discovered that it reflected a consuming interest in music. Each group in his messages represents a letter in a composer's name, and the length of the signal would depend on the spelling. For example if a four-group tuning signal is sent, then we might have guessed it to be

--- --- --- ---

B   A   C H

(Judging by his taste, the signal was unlikely to be B E R G and even more unlikely to be T O C H!) Assuming BACH to be correct, if there were groups common to the first message in subsequent messages we might at least have the basis for making some sense of the content of the plane's reports when these began to be sent. For example : Using our guess to the first message, one might be able to partially decode the next one, if there were groups common to both:

--- --- ---   --- --- ---   --- --- ---

B ? C C H ? ? ? ?

Hurrah – this must be Boccherini giving us a few more letters; and so on. (Victor and I were once involved in a friendly dispute on one group in what was clearly HANDEL to us, when we realised that the Germans had repatriated the great man as HÄNDEL.)

On Being on the Spot

However, assume that all the necessary information is available to decode the messages, reception is good and we are able to track some weather plane somewhere above the Arctic Circle, say at 71° N and 8° E. (Likely as not, our presence there would be as escort for a Russian Convoy. The Flag would be placed in an aircraft carrier and its aircraft, old reliable Swordfish, pushed into the air with rocket-assisted take-off, would offer defensive patrols fed with information about where they might sight enemy aircraft or U-boats.) What role is to be played in the business of protecting our shipping?

Perhaps messages from two weather planes on a North Westerly course from North Norway are being tracked. The crucial question is whether one or both will sight the convoy. The first task is to pinpoint the position of the planes at the time given in their air-to-base messages. At the beginning of their flight they will probably be SE of our position and experience of their direction of flight should enable a prediction to be made as to whether an enemy weather plane will pass South or North or directly over the convoy. It is clearly of importance for the Admiral commanding the convoy escort to know what is the likelihood of being spotted, given his existing estimate of the course he wishes to follow. He might be required to change course in light of the action of the weather plane, which can be affected by the state of the weather. So we have to be constantly on the alert, so long as the planes are aloft, and have to report regularly to the SOO.

But what if it is reported that we are likely to be spotted? It is not our job to decide what action should be taken, but we have a role to play in making clear what are the consequences of any proposed action, despite our lowly rank. We are trained to point out that one obvious course of action may be counter-productive and have an adverse effect on information derived from enemy signals. This is to intercept the plane and shoot it down before it can make a sighting. This has been known to be the first reaction of members of an Admiral's staff, but the Admiral is probably aware from Admiralty briefing that, tempting though this may be, this is ruled out. Two things can go wrong. A crew of a weather plane under attack will probably have time to alert its base that enemy aircraft are attacking it and this alone will warn the *Kriegsmarine* and the *Luftwaffe* that there is an operation in progress and this can be reported quickly to U-boats and strike aircraft. (By 1944, the threat of aircraft strike diminished as the *Luftwaffe* were withdrawing units to concentrate them on the Russian Front and in anticipation of invasion of the European mainland.) Additionally, the question will be raised in the minds of German intelligence about the source of our information. It will be reasonable for them to assume that British intelligence breaks their codes and this would be bound to lead to a re-casting of their methods of ciphering. There is also a moral issue at stake – weather planes are not armed, but this is probably not worth bringing into the equation in the minds of those likely to suffer from its sightings for these can lead to U-boat attacks.

Taking it as given that the weather planes are to be left alone, it is all the more necessary to know where they are and to consider how sightings can be avoided. The first possibility could be that General Winter will be on our side and either the Arctic weather conditions will prevent flying or restrict sorties in some way. Even if the intrepid pilots follow their usual routes, low cloud or snowstorms can reduce visibility and radar apparatus can be restricted in operation. (I can remember convoys where we thought we were bound to be spotted but awful weather conditions saved us.)

The second possibility is to keep on course but to alter speed so the crossover point of the plane will be avoided. This might work when warships alone are conducting an operation and speed could vary up to 25 knots, but in the case of convoys, account has to be taken of the low speeds and lack of flexibility in changing speed open to loaded merchant ships.

The third possibility is to attempt to deceive the enemy by altering course. Clearly, to work, such deception involved a radical course change, and consideration of the consequences of delaying a return to the required course if the operation is to fulfil its purpose. It also assumes that the enemy has no insight into the use of such a strategy, and no information which would indicate what the true purpose of the operation was likely to be. A convoy heading South after clearing Jan Mayen Island (71º N, 08ºW) would present a suspicious sight if the enemy, with knowledge of the sequential nature of our convoy operations, expected a convoy heading North. The fact that interception of enemy signals would not prevent being spotted was far from the end of the story so far as our activities were concerned. In order to take what avoiding action seems necessary to protect a convoy and its escorts, it is vital to know as precisely as possible when a sighting is likely to occur. The sooner we are able to predict the time, the greater the opportunity to make the necessary preparations, such as, for example, the readiness of our carrier planes to carry out anti U-boat patrols, the use of Asdic, and the state of readiness for firing depth charges. Further, the content of the information on sighting transmitted to base and any subsequent instructions from the base to the planes might be useful, placed alongside other information available to the Flag Officer but to which we are not party.

Making our Mark

Once it was established that we were an integral part of the intelligence gathering machine for the operation, we came more directly to the notice of the Staff Officers, including the Admiral. Their experience of our activities would vary and so would their assessment of our usefulness. On several occasions, I recall being tested out by the Staff Officer Intelligence (SOI), usually a three-ringer, by his claiming to be able to check on the accuracy of our information and the conclusions that we deduced from it. We knew that we faced competition because it was possible that UK-based eavesdroppers could also be picking up the same signals, and their findings might be made known to the Flag via the Admiralty. This was commonly the SOI's source and survival of the test became relatively easy because of the inevitable delay caused by clearing secret information to be made available to the Fleet. This meant that the SOI's information was not as up-to-date as ours. But once *rapport* was established Victor and I would frequently be given an appraisal of the overall intelligence available and sometimes asked our opinion on the reliability of part of it.

The above account may suggest that something very dramatic would follow from a sighting. Anyone reading a history of naval intelligence would know that by the end of 1943 and, particularly after the sinking of the *Scharnhorst* and shortly afterwards the crippling of the *Tirpitz*, the likelihood of a gathering of German surface ships to attack convoys or to ward off strikes by the Royal Navy was no longer on the cards. There were still bombers operating in North Norway, but no longer the concentration of force available in the earlier years of the war. The U-boat packs that had harried the Atlantic and Arctic convoys were being withdrawn because of the threat of Allied invasion of the European Mainland. U-boat attacks were still possible but depleted forces made them more spasmodic, and there was a last-ditch attempt to harry the Russian Convoys by making us run the gauntlet of two ranks of U-boats when a convoy reached the Kola Inlet on its last lap to Murmansk.

There were dramatic moments and whatever may actually have been happening to the disposition of the German naval and air force resources in Northern Waters and Norway, an even more complete system of 'eavesdropping' would not have revealed what these were and how they were likely to change. The German naval authorities themselves were not clear in their own minds, for instance, when the more formidable U-boats then under construction with which they hoped to counter their manifest failure to stop convoy operations in the Atlantic and Arctic would be available. Only the benefit of hindsight affords any credence to the argument that the Admiralty displayed risk averseness to a considerable degree in keeping such a large proportion of its resources tied up in Scapa Flow. In consequence, our units were kept at full alert and covered more than 30 separate operations in the last eighteen months of the war in Europe. If we provided positive information only on a few occasions, there was no knowing in advance when these might be.

The Curses of Discomfort and Boredom

As anyone on active service soon realises, the problems of maintaining morale arise not only from the prospect of danger which can actually appear as a blessed relief but also from the other 'enemies'. Being at sea for almost a month in the most appalling weather conditions is not comparable to a pleasant cruise up the Norwegian coast or viewing the wonders of the Northern Wastes. Added to this, as already indicated, bad working conditions hardly helped matters. In this connection I cannot do better than quote from a letter from Morton Andrews, one of my shipmates, who pays me an undeserved compliment: 'We were aboard HMS *Vindex* and our office was the cleared-out flag locker just off the flight deck. Conditions were dreadful, cramped, cold, condensation on the bulkheads from the breath of those working there. You, in your considerate and practical way, used to let us go one at a time on the flight deck for five or ten minutes, if nothing was happening. I stepped out and saw a duffle-coated older man (sans cap). We passed each other a couple of times and then I fell into step beside him saying that it seemed ridiculous not to walk together. He asked the usual, "What are you?". I explained that I was enjoying some fresh air and then had a moan about the conditions under which we were expected to work. You looked out and I said that I would have to go, something must be happening. Once inside our 'office' you asked me what the Admiral had been saying. Ouch! I had assumed that he was a chiefy and then I wondered if keel hauling was still allowed. Moments later there was a knock on the door. We shuffled the chairs along as we had to do to open the door: there was the Admiral complete with cap, together with the Commander. He looked around, looked at me and said, "You did not exaggerate, young man". Next he asked for the ship's carpenter and the Chief Engineer. "Good morning chips, do you think that you could make a duck board for this place?" "Yes sir", and it was done. The Chief Engineer arranged for a device which enabled us to get some ventilation without violating the black-out. An electric fire was fitted to the bulkhead farthest from the door.' I remember thinking that my maternal grandmother was quite right when she used to say, "if you want to get things done, go to the head serang".* The 'head serang' in this case was Vice- Admiral Dalrymple-Hamilton.

It was clearly not always possible to alleviate acute discomfort by appeal to a passing admiral, and in any case admirals were powerless in the face of Nature molesting us with dangerous seas and almost unbearable cold. These familiar miseries of the Arctic were joined by another 'enemy' – boredom. This is nothing unusual in service life between spells of action, but compounded in

HMS Vindex aerial view
(Note: various aerials and armament excised by censor!)

the North by the lack of any expectation of fun and games on shore leave. On arrival in the Kola Inlet, there were few attractions in taking the liberty boat to Vaenga where there were no pubs and only a House of Culture where, festooned with propagandistic leaflets about the joys of Communism, one might rustle up a cup of very strong foul tea. Ingenious methods were used by naval ratings who arrived back drunk from such trips and one puts this down to vigorous bartering of tobacco for vodka and crudely constructed knives. The mood of local military and civilian personnel varies according to prompting from the authorities about the value of our presence, who were suspicious of our commitment to opening the Second Front. There might be nothing unusual in a good-going drunken brawl between Russian and British sailors but the consequences of arrest by naval police for breaches of naval discipline differed on both sides. After one such incident it is alleged that the Russians arrested one of their number, handed over his British opponent for us to deal with and then sent a signal to our Flag Officer which, translated, read: 'We have shot our culprit, what action is being taken with yours?' If true, it is inconceivable that similar action would ever have been contemplated on our side and quite possible that the object of those who hauled him back on board did so hoping to minimize the chances of him even being put on a charge.

Returning to Scapa, unscathed, was a bonus in itself but unless leave was in prospect there was not much to raise the spirits, although brave attempts were made to run dances, concerts and cinema shows at HMS *Proserpine*. To ratings Chatham, Devonport and Portsmouth seemed almost as visions of Paradise alongside the Orkneys, though anyone familiar with these depots would know that this was an extreme case of the illusion of distance leading to enchantment. And as the rationing authorities seem to have difficulty in extending their firm grip beyond the mainland, at least it could be claimed that the food was better. There was actually a lively export trade in eggs packed up in disguised containers and sent home by Royal Mail. There were to be shouts of derision when, towards the end of the war in Europe, an Orkney Egg Controller was appointed to enforce the law.

It would be wholly wrong to give the impression that sailors are purely passive adjusters to the constraints of misery imposed by such circumstances. The old hands on the Lower Deck turn to hobbies of all kinds from wood carving and fancy leatherwork to turning tobacco twist into navy cut and so the hours without action can pass away. Our own younger HO ratings hardly have much time to spend between operations and trips South to Cheadle for re-training and managed to fill in the time without getting into too much trouble. Their confrères based in ships lying at anchor in Scapa were not so well placed. (I felt for them particularly when I met a shore-based C of E Chaplain who confessed to being very disappointed at the poor response to his efforts to run a travelling cinema which went round the fleet. There were such good films for his audiences to enjoy but they did not seem to go much for his attempts to bring a scintilla of culture into their lives. His audience reaction was to demand the showing of films which starred a certain Miss Grable,* whom he had not heard of, whereas he thought they should enthuse over the stylish West End acting in *Dear Octopus*.)

Betty Grable (1918-1973) a well known American actress, singer, dancer and film star with a divine figure and noted particularly for her shapely legs. Appropriately enough, she first came to public attention in the highly successful Astaire/Rogers film Follow the Fleet (1936).

The Eavesdroppers were lucky enough to share a common interest in music. When change permitted meeting up ashore or to have time afloat, some means was usually found to music making. I owe a detailed knowledge of the lower parts of the Linz, Haffner and Prague symphonies of Wolfgang Amadeus to Jack Davies' insistence that we struggled through the piano duet arrangements – I cannot recollect in what corner of Lyness he had found a lonely pianoforte. On several occasions Victor produced a violin. In HMS *Vindex*, I think, we discovered a makeshift chapel with a wheezy harmonium and can credit ourselves with the very first performance above the Arctic Circle of an arrangement for violin and harmonium of Beethoven's *Spring Sonata*. Alan Jay proved to be a very good pianist with a special love for the music of Richard Strauss. We pulled his leg gently by saying that none of us had fully appreciated Strauss's *Ständchen* until we had heard the Great Jay play it. (He induced me some time later to have him accompany my efforts to produce tolerable sounds from my recorder which were presented as one of Handel's Flute Sonatas.)

At sea, and in the Kola Inlet in particular, we were enticed into the Wardroom junketings once its regulars had found that Eavesdroppers were not necessarily wholly eccentric beings. Sometimes we played liar dice in the convivial company of Fleet Air Arm pilots, often younger than ourselves, and then during foul weather when they were on patrol we realised that some of them would not return. With gin at 3d a tot, there were occasions of roistering with the inevitable round of very bawdy songs, actually sung rather well and with astonishing feats of memory when it came to the once unmentionable words. (After some such occasion and feeling very low – we were anchored in the Inlet in a howling gale – Victor and I decided that we should keep our professional skills in practice by preparing German translations. We did not get very far. We started with the wellknown story of Anthony Clare who could perform a remarkable trick with intimate parts of his body – 'with a dexterous twist of his muscular wrist, he could throw them right over his head'. The problem was not only to find the *mot juste* in German, to coin a phrase, but to make the thing rhyme. We never got any further than the first verse – not even the chorus – but suicidal tendencies induced by the eternal night of an Arctic winter were soon dispelled and we had a good laugh. German scholars may now deconstruct our prodigious efforts:

> *'Es war einmal dies' Antony Clare*
> *Ein wunderbarer Zauberer*

Es gab kein Gleich
Im ganzen Reich
Fürs – wait for it – *Hodenverflecterei.'*)

I made one further attempt at trying to use the rationed amount of leisure time. I spotted a Fleet Order that the College of the Sea, a very reputable correspondence college originally set up to help merchant seamen, had extended its activities to include Royal Navy personnel who could enrol in their study courses or use informal tutorial arrangements. I applied for some economics tuition and after a long interval received a letter from Cambridge in writing, as difficult to decipher as my own, containing an offer to comment on a set of agreed essay subjects. My tutor turned out to be A.C. Pigou, recently retired from the Chair of Political Economy at Cambridge and a Fellow of King's College. I was only vaguely aware of his eminence – he was as famous as Keynes in his day and Keynes had studied with him. I could not then and to this day cannot imagine why he undertook this lowly task, but I wrote six essays for him on which he wrote helpful remarks in the margin usually containing some such metaphor as 'you are good at identifying the individual trees but should pay more attention to describing the dimensions of the wood'. The sage comments and related correspondence seemed to indicate that he expected me to be sitting in the deep peace of some equivalent of King's College library with texts in easy reach, whereas my sole resources were a battered copy of Marshall's famous *Principles* and perhaps some native wit and a good memory; and often as not the roll of the ship interfered with my attempt to provide legible copy on an ancient borrowed typewriter. I was too embarrassed to disclose my difficulties. Recounting my experiences in later years to fellow economists, they were astounded to find that Pigou actually agreed to meet me when I was on leave, for he was painfully shy with strangers. I can only imagine the agony that he suffered when I breezed into his rooms and requested further enlightenment than that available in Marshall. He hurriedly pressed into my hands a copy of another book of *Principles*, this time by A.W. Flux, 1906 edition, which puzzled me greatly as it was all about railway rates. Years later I sent him one of my first articles in a professional journal, and he wrote me a charming letter drawing attention to something written by himself on a similar theme and concluding 'I am afraid that I have now turned into a vegetable'. As I write this, I am engaged in writing an article with an Italian colleague, in which his name features prominently and I must be about the same age Pigou was when he wrote those words.

Homeward Bound

The operation over, the escort or the battle group were then released to return to base. With so much written about the excitement engendered by the prospect of mail, maybe leave, and relief at having survived another spell of up to three weeks or more at sea nothing can be added to the familiar story. Victor and I have written our report to be in the Admiral's hands before we go ashore, copied to an amazing list of authorities represented by indecipherable hieroglyphics. Under Victor's tuition I get used to writing with concision and clarity – at least I think I do – but I do not risk the kind of sideswipe that Victor can get away with about the allocation of accommodation. Was I becoming unnaturally cautious, I wonder, and who would read our report and if they did would they prefer the occasional piece of light relief – or was laconicism to be avoided? We never found out because reaction from the recipients was nil – but for the promised use of the Admiral's bathroom.

The trophies and gifts to take to loved ones and impress shipmates were few from Arctic ports of call. Still, the human propensity to truck and barter is manifested in unusual ways. I bought a white fox fur from a Norwegian trapper in Spitzbergen for £5, and was proud of that, but it brought me only misfortune. My young wife was very sweet about it but did not rush to have it made up. I was astonished when I had a visit in Scapa from the Customs and Excise who had heard where we had been and charged me as much duty as the sale price. I hand it to the experienced regulars who sought out and found tins of caviar in North Russia though I felt it inadvisable to question three-ring officers to find out how they paid for it and how they avoided customs duty. It was alleged that most of it landed up in London restaurants who offered generous payment.

But my main reason for dwelling on our return is an occasion where our interception work was of crucial personal importance. Victor, whose home was in South Africa, had great difficulty in being able to file formal requests for home leave rather than leave in the UK. Then once as we were arranging to be ferried ashore from an escort carrier, an urgent signal was sent requesting that Sub Lieut Kanter SANF should report as soon as possible to HMS *Proserpine*. This must be the long-awaited leave chit, so we got him sent ashore as a matter of priority and I remained behind to muster the rest of our party and its gear. It was some hours later before we were able to disembark and I expected that Victor would be well on his way, perhaps leaving some indication of how long his leave would last. I found him in the Wardroom in a state of mild shock but in a mood to give me a graphic and disturbing account of what had happened to him.

As soon as he reached *Proserpine* he was told to report immediately to the office of the Captain of the Base and found himself facing a preliminary investigation into a charge of breaching security. I should explain that officers' outward mail was given to the Mess Secretary and apparently only occasionally did the Staff Officer Intelligence (SOI) exercise his powers of censorship. The SOI contended that Victor had written a letter home which revealed to his parents that he had taken part in a recent action off the Norwegian Coast aboard HMS *Victorious*. This information could be of use to the enemy. The formality of proceedings and the sharp tone of the SOI could have reduced many a junior officer to plead guilty – but they had reckoned without Victor who, on his own account, was seething with anger but well in control of his feelings. What had he to say for himself, if indeed there was anything that he could say – he was asked. Victor's first line of defence was that he accepted the facts but that there had already been a press report about Norwegian coastal attacks and *Victorious* had been listed as taking part. The SOI countered that the press reports did not specify in which particular operations any individual ship had taken part. Then in a flash of inspiration Victor lent forward and asked the Captain, could he assume that he was able to divulge secret information in his own defence? The Captain was clearly not briefed on our sea-going activities and assumed that this was some sort of bluff, but agreed in the expectation that a mere Sub would hardly have access to classified information of any consequence. Victor asked for further reassurance, and this was impatiently agreed – perhaps it was getting close to lunch. "I know", said Victor, "that the Germans know that *Victorious* took part in the particular operation in question". "What! How can you have access to such information?". Victor replied: "Because I decoded the German naval message giving this information myself!" The SOI was then forced to reveal the nature of our work to the Captain who was furious at not having this information before him. Being a sensible man, he admonished Victor for a technical offence, would enter in the ship's log that this had occurred, but no further proceedings would follow – in other words, no court martial. In future, Victor's mail was to be censored by his senior officer before being handed to the Mess Secretary, that is to say by me.

I often wondered what the motives were of the SOI in giving rise to this absurd charade. I suppose that it was annoying for him not to have any jurisdiction over our activities, or perhaps he did not have enough to do to make his job interesting. I hope it did not reveal anti-semitic tendencies but I cannot be sure. What is unique about this occasion was that, as a result of Victor's courage and skill, our very activities as eavesdroppers were instrumental in preventing a very tricky situation – we had the Germans to thank for that.

Chapter 6

VARIETIES OF ARCTIC EXPERIENCE

———

What Use were We?

In trying to recall what happened sixty years ago it is very easy to fall into the trap of exaggerating one's role in what were often very complicated naval operations. Even using a corrective such as examining naval records now released for public scrutiny and available in the Public Record Office or kindly supplied by the Naval Historical Branch of the Ministry of Defence, there is no way short of detailed historical research to be able to identify at what point any information one might have provided had any effect on a particular operation. I can provide no direct documentary evidence which would help matters for, much to my surprise, the files on such operations, while they contain every conceivable kind of signal relating to the progress of a convoy or a shipping strike, do not refer to our efforts. The only exception that I have unearthed related to Headache reports during the Normandy Landings in 1944, and these convey no idea of their impact. That eavesdropping in the Arctic must have been of some use can only be established for the period in which I was employed in that capacity by its continuous use on all major operations and the unexpected recognition of our efforts which were displayed after it was all over.

Convoy Management

I have tried to refresh my memory about three examples of our operational activities, realising the temptation and perhaps the unconscious desire to re-write our mini-history.

The first elaborates some of the detail of convoy protection and associated operations off the Norwegian Coast. The general procedure for protection is well known and fully documented. The convoy would foregather on the West Coast of Scotland and be protected by ships of Western Approaches until the main covering force of an escort carrier in which the Flag Officer Commanding and his staff would serve: maybe two cruisers and a destroyer escort would take over south of the Faroes having sailed from Scapa Flow. In addition, alongside several convoy operations in 1944 and 1945, there were simultaneous air strikes on coastal shipping supplying the German forces in North Norway and particularly during 1944 on the *Tirpitz* in order to prevent it becoming operational. These were launched from an aircraft carrier backed by a battleship such as HMS *Anson* and destroyer forces. This not only strained German naval resources, notably U-boats and strike aircraft, as well as personnel and supplies needed to keep them operational, but diverted resources that might otherwise be transferred to defend *Festung Europa* (Fortress Europe) when the Allies should land in Normandy. I have taken the example of one of the last convoys to Russia and back, known as JW64 outward and RA64 inward, and their approximate routes outward and inward are shown in Chart 2. On examination of Chart 2 what will be striking are the following:

i)   How quickly on the outward journey the convoy is spotted by Zenit, i.e. the weather planes from Trondheim. My recollection is that we gave advance warning of this which enabled the necessary preparations to be made for coping with shadowing and possible attack by JU88s and U-boats.

ii) The concentration of the German attack in the early days of sailing on the torpedo attacks by aircraft who could anticipate our route. The earlier routes of the convoys followed a course to the West of Jan Mayen Island and North of Bear Island. The later route went closer to the Norwegian coast, a decision clearly based on the declining German capability of mounting extensive U-boat and surface attacks after the sinking of the *Scharnhorst* and crippling of the *Tirpitz* and the necessity to transfer U-boats to attack Allied shipping during and after the Normandy invasion. The advantage of shortening the route was the reduction in sailing time, and the disadvantage the reduction in the flying time necessary for JU88s to mount their bombing attacks which could be very effective against slow moving merchant ships unable to take quick avoiding action, though they were often quite well armed. JU88s maintained radio silence as long as possible, and I do not recall us picking up their signals other than in fragmentary form. Still, we could concentrate on trying to predict the path of the weather planes, as previously described.

iii) The appalling periods of weather as we reach the northernmost part of the journey, both in the form of icing up of ships' decks, notably the flight deck of the escort carrier and the hurricane force gales and fog that hinder flying. In the case of RA64, the effect of hurricane force winds and mountainous seas result in the scattering of the returning convoy on two occasions (19th and 23rd February) with consequential difficulties in reforming the convoy before ships could be picked off by dive bombers. Furthermore, there are only two or so hours of daylight, which makes communication difficult. Of course, particularly bad weather restricts enemy action. Surprisingly, we are kept busy because sometimes weather planes fly in atrocious conditions – and sometimes do not make it back to their home base – though they are not so likely to spot us. We obtain some idea of the extent of their operations because we learn to differentiate between tuning signals including fake messages and genuine communication with weather planes.

iv) The concentration of U-boats at the entrance to the Kola inlet is implicit in the entries on both entering and leaving the Inlet. Our response is to form up the convoy in line ahead and place warships on their flanks which depth charge our way in and out. This can continue for some hours. This is where there are casualties on both sides, with U-boats picking off stragglers and sinking one of our destroyers and in retaliation we attack and sink at least one U-boat. (I am unable to complete the gruesome inventory of loss from the data available but the general nature of the battles to get the entering convoy safely to Murmansk and a small number of merchant ships detached for Archangel and the leaving convoy out to the open sea is surely clear.) This is the time when our eavesdropping activities virtually cease and, as we are on the escort carrier which has no depth charge armament, we are in much the same position as the merchant ships, and come to understand more exactly their hopes and fears. We just have to grit our teeth and keep up our spirits as best we can, which is difficult if one has no positive role to play.

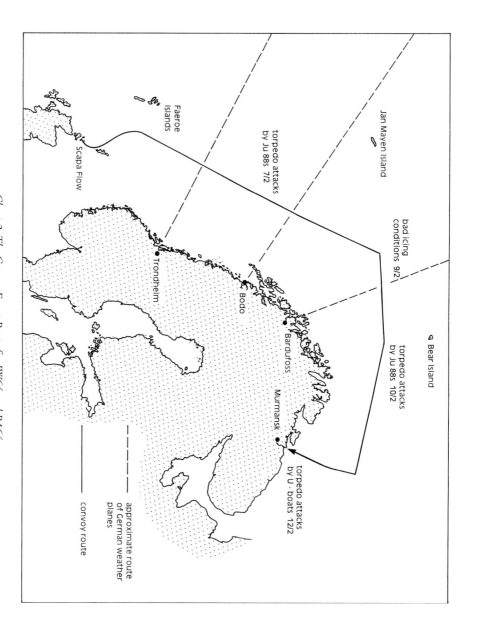

Chart 2. The Convoy Escort Route for JW64 and RA64

Bear Island

torpedo attacks
by Ju 88s 10/2

bad icing
conditions 9/2

Jan Mayen Island

torpedo attacks
by Ju 88s 7/2

Faeroe
Islands

Scapa Flow

Trondheim

Bodø

Bardufoss

Murmansk

torpedo attacks
by U - boats 12/2

approximate route
of German weather
planes

convoy route

This bare narrative of events shows how convoy management was a complicated and intensive activity with no let-up throughout the whole passage from the UK. However, it is only a record of events and can give no feel for the continuing problems encountered in matching expectations as to where and when we would engage the enemy and the skill of those in charge of operations in how to cope with the unexpected. To repeat a previous point the greatest surprise to me in examining the records – and this is the crucial reason for providing this narrative – is how little eavesdroppers knew about what was going on. In reading the memoirs of those who were engaged on decrypting activities at Bletchley, time after time they referred to their puzzlement over how their skills were actually translated into information of use to the war effort. We were perhaps better placed than they were and at least aware that our information could affect decisions about the deployment of escort forces, but I cannot recall any occasion where it was considered necessary to give us a general appraisal of the plan of action of those in charge. It may be that on a 'need to know' basis there was no case for doing so, a good principle when revealing information which would not improve efficiency, but I have often wondered whether we might not have been more useful if we had known more. But this is a clear case of *post hoc ergo propter hoc*, for none of us ever thought of raising this issue, though that might have been difficult enough for very junior 'pigs'.

Far from the Second Front

The second example is more in keeping with the wartime experiences of most of us, that is as a pawn moved around in apparently random fashion to fit in with the immediate and often totally unpredictable demands of strategy. We are back in 1944 after a rest from convoy work and expecting that our expertise would be required in the opening of the Second Front. But the call back to the English Channel, seared on my memory by the Tunnel disaster, never came. Our team was stuck in Scapa and while in retrospect we should have regarded ourselves as lucky, we felt cheated and rather guilty at not being part of the Invasion. What were you doing, Dad, on the great day? It is literally true that I was invited aboard HMS *Rodney* where some eccentric officer had organized a dinner where we were supposed to appear in naval mess dress – which I certainly did not possess – and actually bribed (I suppose) a few members of the remains of a Band of the Royal Marines to play Songs from the Shows while we solemnly ate an excuse for a meal and drank toasts in decent port of varying degrees – to me – of obscurity which harked back to the 'real' Navy of peacetime. The 'band' consisted of three rather bemused and out of practice musicians and a conductor who bobbed up and down in time in an attempt to simulate the concerts of better days. I should have been cheered by this morale building effort and grateful to meet battle scarred veterans of previous naval actions, but, returned to *Proserpine* in the ship's tender, puzzled and depressed.

Then after a very brief visit to Cheadle Victor and I were surprised to find ourselves mysteriously dispatched as quickly as possible to Greenock but arrived a day or two earlier than we were expected, and sworn to secrecy about our movements. There was enough time to enjoy a walk in the hills behind Gourock but the signal event before embarkation was a chance visit to Glasgow where I managed to obtain a ticket to see the famous Kurt Jooss perform the dance of death in *The Green Table*. Its theme may be the futility of war and the hypocrisy of diplomats but its interest for me lay less in the message and more in the drastic contrast between expressionist ballet which it represents and classical ballet's use of virtuosity, which it rejects. This cultural interval was soon pushed quickly into the past by the sight at Greenock of a cruiser with destroyer escort alongside to which were tied several landing craft which were being loaded up by Norwegian soldiers. So that was it – we were going to take part in a diversionary invasion force making for Norway, and this would more than fulfil our desire to join the action so far denied us. It so happens that immediately after the war in Europe was over I was asked to write a short piece on my naval experiences. It was commissioned for the Dundee High School Magazine by George Bruce, then my former English master, who became one of Scotland's most distinguished contemporary poets. I reproduce it here, not because I think it has any particular literary merit, but because it shows what I picked out at the time as being of interest about the Norwegian 'invasion' which turned out to be nothing of the sort. Remember that this is a lad of 23 writing who has so far never produced anything in print. There is another purpose in reprinting it that will soon become apparent.

Dear Mr Bruce

What a task you have set me! Unfortunately their Lordships at the Admiralty did not let me keep a diary of day-to-day events, but I'm rather glad in a way, because many of the entries would be monotonous monosyllabic half-mutterings – 'snow' or 'cold and wet.' Brrr! However, let me tell you about one of the brighter moments when we weren't bucketing up and down the Murmansk 'club run' and when we had more consolation than just the thought that U-boats and aircraft chasing us were having just as bad a time as ourselves. Let me tell you instead about Longyearby. (78 degrees 12 min. N., 15 degrees E.)

Now that you've found it, on the Atlas behind your desk, nestling in the upper niche of cleft Spitzbergen, just repeat the name again. Doesn't it sound enchantingly mysterious? Long-year-by – I've never dared to find out what it meant in case I suffered the awful disillusionment of years ago when I first repeated 'Erehwon' backwards! But it is just about the last place on the road to nowhere, and when you glide up on the tip of the Gulf Stream's tongue, past the towering ice mountain on the port hand and into Ice Fiord, you enter a land of mystery and Longyearby is its gateway.

What do people do, stuck up there? There are people there, I suppose, you ask? Long years back they discovered coal at Longyearby. You could just pick it off the ground like pebbles off a beach. So they sent miners from North Norway and the coal went back to supplement the scarce wood fuel in Tromsö and Hammerfest. (They tried to export the coal to Scotland, but when they opened the holds at Methil there was only coal dust there!) When the Germans occupied the Norwegian mainland in 1940, our friends across the North Sea had one little spot left which belonged to them. They kept a small garrison to look after the mines, collect valuable meteorological and other information which they transmitted to Great Britain. They took a pride in still being on native soil.

But to be garrisoned there too long had its dangers. In 1940 they had to set the mines on fire in case the Germans came. They are smouldering to this day. In 1943 the *Scharnhorst* and *Tirpitz* came out for some target practice at the mining installations by Longyearby's tiny jetty. The battleships opened up with their secondary armament. A single Oerlikon gunner raked their decks from the foreshore. In August, 1944, a U-boat surfaced in the Ice Fiord and sent a landing party ashore, but they were beaten off; the only damage caused was to a small motor-boat, but it was their only one. So when the ice line receded to the North Pole crest, and the days got longer, we sent reliefs and supplies, and took back those who had lived through the winter of perpetual night.

That's why I happened to go there. About a fortnight after D-Day, when my friend K. and I had got over the disappointment at not being in the Channel, we found ourselves looking over the stern on a 6-in. cruiser in the Forth of Clyde. We had already noticed the Norwegians on board; our eyes were following the lay of a hawser towards what appeared to be confirmation of our speculations about this trip – two landing craft! However, it wasn't a second invasion after all. It was to be a real Arctic expedition as we soon found out. Further examination revealed food packing cases, medical stores and all sorts of paraphenalia which made H.M.S. J— look rather like her untidy cousin, a cargo ship. The relief troops lined the guard rails, paced the deck or sprawled over their piles of gear playing cards. Most of them had been to Spitz before, some were the miners of the island in khaki disguise. They were killing time. They were impatient.

It took us five days; weather fine, sea and swell moderate, no confirmed U-boat contacts and German aircraft carefully but neatly dodged. This was a fast job at 22 knots, based on an official zigzag course with scope for all the embellishments of high-speed manoeuvre that the *"straight ringers"** revel in. The captain rubbed his hand at all the extra work he was giving our destroyer escort as they jockeyed into quarter line or fell astern to form up in line ahead. This was the real stuff after convoys, where a senior officer might have to fly his flag in one of those dreadful converted 'banana boats' – the escort carriers! But most of us were content at being on an adventurous, 1800 mile trip at 16 knots more than we were used to, and a certain pride at going further north than any of our cruiser squadron had ever been.

Our only visitor in the whole of our wide sweep across that frightening expanse of cold sea was a Greenland Owl, that huge bird with talons long enough to gore a rabbit and a wingspan approaching that of a Ju.88. (We thought it was one at first.) He touched down, exhausted, on our spinning radar aerial, 300 miles from the nearest piece of land, having picked on possibly the only bit of shipping in 14,000 square miles of the Arctic. It flew off the next day when it saw the great glacial tower in the distance at the entrance of Ice Fiord. It disappeared towards the north-east, to where the expectant garrison would be watching on the quay at Longyearby, as they would have been for days now, listening in the silence for the throb of our engines.

The bird was our messenger.
They would now soon know of our coming.

How tight-lipped can you get? The piece shows just how conditioned one had become to security reinforced by being in Intelligence and therefore with the *Official Secrets Act* engraved on the memory. 'K' is of course Victor Kanter, and 'J' is HMS *Jamaica*. The unidentified captain is the formidable Captain J. Hughes-Hallett scandalously slandered together with his brother of similar seniority, as Hughes-Hitler and Hughes-Himmler. There is a reference to German aircraft 'carefully and neatly dodged' which is as near to, or as far from, one felt able to get to a mention of our job. On both this and a repeat performance in September 1944, Victor and I and our team earned their corn.

There were other features of this sortie to the extremities of navigable waters in the North which seem worth a mention. The opportunity afforded to Captain Hughes-Hallett to demonstrate the naval equivalent of the most polished form of precision movement must have been irresistible, and indeed it was a lesson to HOs* to watch the various forms of manoeuvre which occupied so much of the peacetime Navy. But Victor and I, apart from our own work in which the Captain took a considerable interest, were not exempted from his desire to have us all smartened up after the more informal atmosphere of the flight deck of an escort carrier slowly ploughing the seas to Murmansk. Like all officers we were expected at all times to wear the regulation collar and tie, particularly on the bridge in the Captain's presence. Our constant movement back and forward from ship to shore and ship again played havoc with laundry arrangements. Victor overcame these by covering his open-necked shirt with a smart scarf made up to look like a cravat whereas I relied on using a duffel coat as a cover-up so that one could save collar and tie, only used on coming on board or going ashore. Our problems were solved in exactly the same way as those of most of the junior officers aboard. The Navigating Officer did a roaring trade by producing cut-out collars made from old charts. These were issued at bargain prices with two warnings. The first was that with extended use, they were apt to fray and the peaks would turn up, revealing on the reverse side their origins in the form of the navigational markings found on all charts. One had therefore to invest in a considerable supply of them to last a week at sea. The second was never to go down to the engine room wearing such a collar, for the sudden rise in temperature on entry would cause it to disintegrate. But nothing I have said is meant to malign Captain Hughes-Hallett. He was a man of proven worth and if reared in the firm mould of good order and naval discipline, the acid test was his professional skill which he fully demonstrated in both sorties to Spitzbergen. And on our departure he sent for us and thanked us, seeming, despite his formidable presence, to be rather shy.

The garrison had run short of liquor before our arrival because of the uncertain nature of relief arrangements. As we sailed out of Bell Sound, a Norwegian army doctor enquired about the availability of whisky and bought a duty free bottle from the Wardroom, then disappeared to his bunk to make short work of it. We did not see him for 48 hours.

This account would seem very dated to the hundreds of tourists for whom Spitzbergen has been 'done' and is no longer on the list of luxury cruises which denote travellers who rely on exclusivity as a mark of their social status. The cruises penetrate ever further north. My notion of the romance and mystery of 'Longyearby' has been shattered. It is simply the crude phonetics of the name of some long-dead explorer called, I believe, Longair. The shanty settlement of long ago serving as a mining camp has been gentrified and all the accoutrements which the well-off tourist expects are now available. But this 'lad', now over 80, still holds to his vision of a strange land and can perhaps more easily appreciate, having been in Arctic waters in winter months, the mystery of the Aurora Borealis and perpetual night, where few tourists will linger until the winter to enjoy and in peace.

Moving to the Attack

Convoy protection and garrison relief seem only gestures towards the continuance of a naval tradition stretching back for centuries, and a long way from engaging the enemy at close quarters, first with shot and then using grappling irons to bring them within the range of pistol fire and cutlasses as seen in so many thirties and forties films with Errol Flynn in the thick of it fighting for the honour of Queen Bess. I should have mentioned that before I was called up I did make an abortive attempt to join the Marines after seeing some propaganda film. I volunteered and realised that I would fail the eyesight test, unless I could find some means of finding out which eyesight chart would be used and enough time to memorize it. I arrived somewhat early at the Caird Hall, Dundee where the medical was to be held and found it deserted, sneaked into the sight testing unit and took a note of the eye chart. When my turn came to be tested I was able to read the top four lines without difficulty and my memory served me well on the rest, remembering that suspicions would be aroused if I could read the last line correctly. After I left the booth, I saw the optician swivel the chart – my luck had held. One of the medical board had been on the naval board and knew me as a member of the same church congregation and I thought I had been found out. No. He accepted my reasons for wanting to volunteer and wished me well. But the Royal Navy called me up before the Marines could confirm my acceptance as one of them, and refused to let me transfer. It was providential. I cannot imagine that I could ever have led a landing party of Marine Commandos, and would have been horrified to have served, as many did, as officers' servants on battleships though I might have been trained as a woodwind player in a Marine Band. (The farcical occasion when I did lead a posse of Marines boarding a German ship is another story reserved for later description!)

After the sinking of the *Scharnhorst* in December 1943, the Home Fleet was in a better position to mount attacks on shipping off the Norwegian coast, concentrating on getting rid of the potential menace of the last remaining German battleship in the Arctic, the *Tirpitz*. I was 'blooded' in the first of these attacks in early 1944, serving on the *Royalist* as the Flagship, but our team did not pick up any messages which had a direct bearing on the action. Things were different in April when a carrier-borne aircraft attack on *Tirpitz*, now in Kaa Fjord in North Norway, was carried out from two fleet carriers and four escort carriers which put *Tirpitz* out of action but did not sink her. It was not known at the time that she was virtually beyond repair so that further attacks were mounted later in the year. The April operations were commanded by Vice-Admiral Sir Henry Moore, then Second in Command of the Home Fleet, known as VA2.

This was the first occasion when I came face to face with such a high ranking officer, and I was understandably apprehensive when called at the double from our crowded and uncomfortable office to be cross-questioned about a report I just sent to his staff claiming that our strike force would soon be sighted by a German weather plane. I arrived on the bridge of the *Anson* in which, as I have explained, I was a temporary member of the Gun Room, and found myself, this raw 22 year old, confronted by the full gamut of gold braid from three ringers to the two rows of 'scrambled eggs' which graced the peak of VA2's cap. Sensing my apprehension at being arraigned before his formidable staff, VA2 in a quiet voice asked me a few personal questions and then quizzed me on my evidence, and I soon realised that I would be neither barked at nor bitten. After a brief consultation with his impressive entourage, and before dismissing me, VA2 ordered the strike force to alter course 180 degrees, so that on sighting we would appear to be steering a south westerly and not a north easterly course. I could hardly maintain my delight at the idea that eavesdropping could have such a decided effect on the course of the action, though soon tempered by the thought that I might be deprived of my commission if I was proved wrong. Fortunately, the sighting took place as expected, and the weather plane gave no indication that this manoeuvre was an exercise in deceit. (Sometimes I wonder if this was not an invention of my own, and I have not been able to consult the log of *Anson*. A mention would be unlikely in the Summary of Service of *Anson* which is available from naval records and this proved to be the case. What I did discover over fifty years after the event is that this was not the first time that Henry Moore had used this dodge in Arctic waters, but whether in response to similar intelligence information I do not know.)

By the end of 1944 it was realised that the crippled *Tirpitz* was no longer a menace to convoys and to our own strike forces. A cruiser such as *Devonshire*, which played a major part in covering air strikes against the *Tirpitz*, was transferred from escort work for aircraft and escort carriers to the more aggressive role of strikes against coastal shipping carrying supplies up the Norwegian Coast and minelaying activities. This also extended the coverage of our own operations, and on several occasions the four of us were split up and were paired by an RAF NCO from Cheadle to keep up the supply of eavesdropping. All of them were experienced men but only one or two had sea time behind them, and the secondment to the Arctic was a new, unexpected adventure. Just before

Christmas 1944 one such very tall NCO came with me and the usual party of W/T operators to join this famous three-funneller with a wide beam which had seen service and action in both the South Atlantic and Indian Ocean. For once we had enough space to stow my gear and between watches I began writing my first essay for Professor Pigou on my battered typewriter. This was an assignment where it was quite possible that our usefulness would depend less on anticipating sightings but more on listening for messages transmitted between shore stations and between such stations and attacking aircraft. Our strikes were aimed at shipping in the Trondheim area and were a strong reminder of my service in the Channel but this time fairly confident that the strike force would not be scattered before firing a shot. And so it turned out to be.

There was little to report on the outward run, but by great luck we picked up messages, some of them in low grade code and practically *en clair* which clarified the enemy's appraisal of our strength and warned us in advance that the JU88 torpedo bombers would be after us. The JU88s made three runs but it was dark before they could reach us and although it is not a pleasant experience listening for their approach, this was drowned in the formidable barrage of gunfire put up by *Devonshire* and its escorts. We returned home having shot down a JU88 and the mission accomplished without loss.

I cannot associate the officers commanding the various operations described with the common perception of men of impulsive action trying to emulate Nelson at the Battle of Aboukir Bay. All of them, including the genial and vigorous Captain Bain DSO of the *Devonshire*, had enviable records in action but perhaps lacked the opportunity during the time I encountered them to display inspirational qualities in close encounters with enemy forces. That is probably as well, for dash and daring might be more a hindrance than a help in keeping a close eye on the positioning of naval craft, particularly on convoy work. The greater opportunities for becoming attacking forces soon involved us in an action which was consonant with what are perceived as the activities of gallant sailors. At very little notice, one of our units, with myself in charge, together with Jack Davies as Headache officer, were bundled aboard HMS *Kent* one cold November day in 1944 in which Rear Admiral Roderick McGrigor had hoisted his pennant as Commander of the 1st Cruiser Squadron which included one cruiser, HMS *Bellona*, and four destroyers. The Admiral was obviously delighted at being in charge of a surface attack on enemy shipping which involved going close inshore off the Lister Fjord in the South West corner of Norway, and in his address to us as we steamed away at 20 knots from Scapa betrayed the characteristics of a seadog off the leash.

The official summary account of operation 'Counterblast' – a title clearly indicating a turn of events in Arctic operations – despite its observing the proprieties of naval reporting – cannot avoid conveying the vigour and enthusiasm of the Admiral's response to his task:

'On the night of the 12th (November), the force intercepted an enemy convoy in 58° 14N, 06° 12E., off the Lister Fjord, south-east of Egersund. It included about 11 ships, of which three or four were escorts, including M-class minesweepers. Complete surprise was achieved, and it is believed that all the enemy ships were blown up or sunk, except possibly one merchant ship and one escort, of which one may have run ashore. Several shore batteries joined in the later stages of the action and were "spectacular, but ineffective". No major damage was sustained by the British ships, and apart from minor injuries there were two killed and five wounded in the *Verulam* and two wounded in the *Kent*.'

Things were a good deal more exciting and angst-giving than the report is able to convey. The operation really began by our forces creeping through a minefield. Then McGrigor marshalled his forces and when in sight of the enemy convoy and escort brought them into line ahead* and gave the order to open fire on the enemy when we were in parallel with them. But that was not all. The Nelson touch came by placing his forces not to seaward of them but landward so that we were steaming between the convoy and the shore. This must have certainly confused the enemy but once it was surmised what McGrigor was up to, he would be courting two dangers. The first was that we were brought within easy firing range of the coastal shore batteries, the second that we had to be careful not to run aground. McGrigor was contemptuous of the risks and his luck held. The shore batteries took a long time to realise what was happening, indicating that the attack was a complete surprise; the *Kent's* navigator had simply to keep his fingers crossed. And, as the official account indicates, running ashore was not only a risk but became the likely fate of one of the enemy vessels.

Our part in the action must now be reluctantly recorded. The team was placed in a large storage area beneath the after 8 inch gun turret which would also have to serve as the ratings' sleeping quarters. Not that sleep would be guaranteed anyone if we were at action stations all night. The equipment was set up and tested as we made our way to the point of attack and all was well. There was no relevant W/T traffic and we did not expect any until action started when both Headache R/T and our W/T wavelengths might yield some ship-shore communication. As soon as the guns above us fired, there was chaos. The strong vibration caused most of our sets to lose their moorings and then there was a blackout and a complete power cut. We were completely immobilised and there was no way we could ourselves restore power and resume eavesdropping. There is nothing more likely to unsettle crew in a surface action than to have nothing to do. We just had to wait in the dark until the action was over and to hope that we were out of range and out of the firing line of the shore batteries. However, someone had to know that we could not deliver. Leaving the leading hand in charge, I made a dash along the deck to report what had happened to the SOO and to seek instructions. Just keep your head down and make the best of it was the reply and back I went, watching what was becoming like a firework display with the exchange of fire. I have never been completely easy about the lighting up of the night sky on Guy Fawkes night ever since. The characteristic cheerfulness of our team returned remarkably quickly as we made it back to Scapa. It was not our fault at least that we had not shared in the glories of battles and that others had saved our skins.

Chapter 7

AFTERMATH

———

Home is the 'Sailor'

The escorting ships for the last Russian convoy arrived back in Scapa just before the war in Europe was officially declared as over. It was a curious homecoming. There was a relaxed atmosphere on board HMS *Vindex* and Rear Admiral Cunningham-Graham, yet another Scot alongside his senior admirals, Fraser, Dalrymple-Hamilton and McGrigor, metaphorically hid his gold braid and chatted amicably with me about our respective roles and our curious experiences. The only incident of potential danger was the rescue of some fleeing citizens of Kirkenes far up in North Norway when their town was set on fire by the retreating Germans. Their evacuation was carried out by destroyer escorts and the wounded or ill who escaped were taken aboard *Vindex*, which had the best equipped sick bay. I was asked to see if I could make myself understood to one particular casualty, a very old (it seemed) Finnish lady who was bedridden. Verbal communication was soon abandoned but she expressed her delight and surprise at rescue by crooning and nodding her head. She sat up in bed and smiled at everyone, with a handsome, gentle countenance – everyone's Mum. And so it turned out to be. The word got around the mess decks about our visitor and hardened sailors queued up to visit her, some with well-meant but unsuitable gifts, including drink; and strong men wept.

And then, as suddenly as it had begun, we were rapidly dispersed. It was as if we had been members of a troupe of strolling players bound by the necessity of having to play particular roles in a long dramatic performance in which we had learnt in detail our virtues and failings and to rub along together and so tied to what we were immediately doing that we could not envisage any other sort of life. The war must end just like any long theatre run but one was frequently in the mood when one thought it would last for ever and, like the crew captained by the Flying Dutchman, in the Middle Watch on a freezing Arctic night one might be reduced to the misery of thinking we would remain perpetually at sea. But sharing one's miseries and one's minor triumphs, when something we did made our role seem to have a purpose and helped us to tolerate the uncertainty as to when the show would end; and there would be many who on returning to civvy street would, like Byron's Prisoner of Chillon, regain their freedom with a sigh.

La Commedia e Finita and we are assigned new roles in other theatres, not of war perhaps but to deal with its aftermath. Kanter, Jay, Horder, Davies and I speculated on the possibility that we would meet again in the Far East, retrained to cover Japanese signalling, but the dropping of the atomic bomb in August 1945 put paid to that and we were left in Europe filling appointments in the Naval occupation of Germany where our German might be useful. But that is another story and this glimmering of its contents is only meant to show how quickly we were confronted with adjustment to a different order of things, in which the informality and unorthodox nature of our sea-going activities would be at a discount, and before we were demobilised we might find ourselves having to come to terms with the stricter routines and customs of the peace-time Navy which the regulars began to talk about. Kanter would not then get away with a yellow scarf disguised as a cravat and I would have to wear my 'titfer' at a more orthodox angle.

Then the order for 'demob' came unexpectedly and I found myself released under the Class B system which favoured release of students who had not completed their studies; a surprise, because with the number 44 attached to my demob ranking I thought I would still be in Kiel Harbour seizing German ships in prize for at least another year.

The way of saying God speed in the Royal Navy, other than in the form of farewell parties in the Ward Room, would strike those of the age I was then – scarcely 23 – as amounting to the bum's rush. No 'de-briefing' with others going back into the wicked world; no attempt to offer counselling to enable us to live with our harrowing experiences of the past (thank God!); no lectures and seminars on the perils of going back into civilian life, with advice on how to run one's finances and make claims for benefits; no foregathering at the Admiralty DSD 9 Branch for a kiss goodbye. But then we did not expect anything of the kind and we were simply glad to be leaving more or less sound in mind and limb and no doubt their Lordships believed that, even as only erstwhile naval officers, we would have learnt how to fend for ourselves. Roll on the trip to Olympia in West Kensington for the issue of civvies, including jacket and pork pie hat, a savings bank book with a small gratuity, and two weeks' paid leave before final release. I was back at the University of St Andrews as an Honours undergraduate by mid-October, with the official date of release as 29th October, the day after our first child, David, was born. My status had been eroded, and simultaneously my responsibilities increased; not to speak of the plunge back into a world of awesome contemplation with a first essay on the Concept of the Social Contract in the work of Hobbes and Locke to finish by the middle of term.

Before the essay was due, there was a curious atmosphere to contend with in being some of the first of the returning 'heroes'. The University authorities, though not the bulk of the academic staff who could not have been more considerate and understanding about helping us to settle in, appeared to be worried in case a legacy of belligerence remained amongst us and we would take the place apart. At least that was the impression gained when six of us were asked to see the Secretary of the University shortly after we had exchanged service kit for the Scarlet Gown of our Alma Mater. I remembered him as a rather lowly official, the Bursar of a College, but in the course of three years, saved from conscription and living in a place almost untouched by war, he had moved rapidly through the bureaucratic ranks to become the Principal's mouthpiece. I do not recall being asked to sit down in the Secretary's office; in fact I am fairly sure that we were left standing while Mr Ritchie, known to us previously as 'Piggie', asked us to listen carefully. The Principal, Sir James Irvine, to whom apparently we owed our early release, wanted it to be known that the University expected in return we would remember that we were once again '*in statu pupilari*' and rumbustious behaviour would not be tolerated. We would also be expected, if we had been scholars, to forfeit our claim to scholarships for we would all have been awarded ex-service study grants. Here we were, four of us married, three with families to support, and anxious to make up for lost time, treated in a manner which we would never have had to tolerate whilst in the services. The Principal's fears would have been realised at the very moment of their promulgation had our anger matched our contempt.

Fortunately, other persons in authority had more confidence in us. Later on after some brush between the students and the disciplinary authorities, I recall one Professor arguing that, in his opinion, the law of master and servant was applicable to the case of undergraduates. I exploded and interjected: "You don't employ us, we employ you". We were both wrong in law, I believe, but our argument led to no recrimination. Indeed, I owe and am very grateful to the same Professor, Wilkie Nisbet, for offering me my first academic appointment.

I have exaggerated what appeared to be the Navy's austere farewell; in fact I have been unfair. Just before I received my marching orders, I had a short spell of leave during which I heard that Allan Jay had been awarded a decoration and I commented on this to the Accounting Officer of RNTE Southmead, whom I met by chance on a bus going down Putney Hill. He stared at me and accused me of fishing for compliments and when, puzzled, I asked him to explain himself he said, angrily, "Well, what about your DSC?" I had difficulty in convincing him that this was the first I had heard about it. I leapt off the bus at the bottom of the Hill and rang The Admiralty who read out the citation of the award gazetted on 12th July, confirmation of which would be waiting for me in Kiel. 'For skill, resourcefulness and determination on special service with the Home Fleet' it read and there were the names of Allan and myself as now holders of the Distinguished Service Cross and the award of the Distinguished Service Medal to CPO Marsland and L/T Skipworth. When I returned to Kiel there was a letter of congratulation from the Director of Naval Intelligence, who was not identified, and understandable surprise amongst the real sailors at Kiel. I shared and still share that surprise for I had no claim to have done anything brave or courageous for which the DSC is generally awarded. More modest souls would have kept it quiet but not having much to show for what I had done in life, I added the ribbon to my row of medals. Today when published after my name it is commonly mistaken for Doctor of Science.

When about to be demobbed I was called to a Naval Medical Centre in Queen Anne's Gate, London for what turned out to be a full medical examination. This was made necessary because of my Wound and Hurt Certificate and therefore the possibility that I might claim a War Pension, which had never occurred to me. The Surgeon Commander was thorough and brusque, and seemed to find me in the peak of physical condition, until he examined my right ear. "You have a perforation in this ear", his voice undergoing a quick crescendo, "when did this happen?". "At birth", I explained.

He gave me an astonished look: "My God", he almost shouted, "if I had examined you on entry you would never have been admitted to the Royal Navy". The months of struggle, discomfort and disappointment rather than the things that I enjoyed swam before my eyes. Knowing I would be out in days, I am ashamed to say that respect for authority deserted me and I offered the cheeky riposte: "And this, Sir, if I may say so, is a bloody fine time to be told that". He sniffed and sent me away.

Reminders

Many servicemen willingly chain themselves to their past war-time experiences and join and meet regularly at various ex-service organizations. They look back on the days when they had a distinct common purpose to survive and defeat the enemy and enjoyed the comradeship of adversity. My generation struggle on to attend Armistice parades, throw back their shoulders and march in step, supporting comrades who no longer are able to walk, and reluctantly accepting, as their ranks inevitably get thinner, that they may soon have to hold their last gathering. It is hardly to my credit that I have never attended such occasions. I was not even aware until I was sent the Order of Service that Morton Andrews and others who had served with me had been present on Maritime Sunday 2000 at a Commemoration of the Battle of the Atlantic, and they had taken part in the March Past. (Recalling my previous attempts to get them to march in step, I wondered how they performed!). Explanations are possible but not excuses. The nature of 'Y' and Intelligence work at sea did not encourage long and close contact with one group of people, and the *Official Secrets Act* inhibited the sharing of experiences. There were many competing substitutes in later life in professional associations and in family matters, and academics tend to be nomads. I did enrol in the RNVR Officers Supplementary Reserve, but this entailed no duties, and I resigned in late 1956. It looked like an act of cowardice for, purely by chance, my resignation coincided with the Suez Crisis; but there was never any prospect that I would have become involved in it.

However, I have never resisted when my navy past has tugged at my sleeve through some chance event. This began just before I was demobbed. I managed to make a quick diversion on the journey South from Scapa to Cheadle by slipping off the train at Perth and finding a convenient train to Dundee. My parents, though glad to see me, seemed in a conspiratorial mood.

Then my mother said, "Go into your old room and you will find something interesting". It was my 'ditty box' which I had thought had been stolen from me at Charing Cross Station three years before. I opened it. There was my pay book, clean sailor collar, small towel and bar of soap. Not a thing was missing. Incredibly, a merchant seaman had picked up my small brown case which was identical to his own and rushed for a train. His gain was as despairing as my loss to me, but he held on to it, identified the owner and next of kin (with address) from my pay book. After sailing twice round the world, purely by chance his ship came to land some cargo in Dundee docks, and he handed the case over to the local 'stone frigate' and in turn the officer-in-charge of it contacted my parents. My case had seen more of the world than I had.

About six years later I read in the *Evening Standard* that an ex-naval officer had shot himself in a forest near the German-Belgian border. He was on the run and suspected of having murdered his wife and mother-in-law. His name was Chesney, and it transpired that as a boy he had appeared in the Court of Session in Edinburgh in the 1930s charged with the murder of his mother – the verdict was not proven. I simply could not believe that this was the jolly rumbustious two-ringer, with a different sort of ring in his ear, who had descended on HMS *Proserpine* one winter evening and entertained us with stories of his chequered career in Motor Torpedo Boats. His was a tour-de-force which would long be remembered by his admiring audience. But then on reading of his miserable demise, I remembered one disturbing feature during his performance. He would produce a dagger from his pocket and occasionally punctuate his stories by throwing it at some nearby wooden surface such as a bar table or just the bare floor.

Not long afterwards, I opened the same paper and read an account of the appeal by Field Marshal Kesselring against sentence of death. He had, of course, commanded the German troops during their hardly-fought retreat in the face of the Allied landings in Sicily and later Italy. The principal witness for the defence was a Lieutenant Colonel Scotland and I remembered meeting him not long after I was demobbed. My naval experience had enabled me to obtain a vacation post in 1946 as a tutor at Wilton Park, where German prisoners of war were given lectures on current affairs, preparatory to return to their war-torn country. The tutors were made members of the officers' mess in the country house and there I met this rather elderly visiting army officer whose name denoted his origins. He came from Perth only 20 miles from my home and both aware of our background in intelligence carefully avoided any discussion of official secrets. Instead we had a heated but friendly argument about the Malthusian views on population growth, which he espoused and I did not. It was only some time later that it was let slip to me that the country house in the grounds of which we were running our courses was the jailhouse of captured German generals.

Victor, you may remember, was forced to defend himself by having to reveal very sensitive information about his intelligence activities. The British officers acting for Kesselring's defence were permitted to reveal much more astonishing and sensitive information by calling Lieutenant Colonel Scotland. On cross-examination he was presented as if he had been a spy who had infiltrated the German Waffen SS and had become an officer in Kesselring's army! He testified that Kesselring's treatment of Allied prisoners of war was fair and just and his testimony was probably a major factor in saving Kesselring, who was pardoned and later released. Scotland wrote a most interesting book about his activities in which he reveals that the War Office refused to let him elaborate on how he had become bilingual.

The last formal contact with the Royal Navy was to mark the end of an old naval tradition. My final posting, now promoted to Lieutenant RNVR, was as Assistant Prize Officer at the naval base at Kiel. My task was to board surrendered merchant ships, overcome any show of resistance and formally seize them in prize. On the first occasion that I did so I arrived on board a large cargo boat with a posse of Royal Marines, all of us armed, and the German skipper looked at us and laughed: "*Was is los, Junge; Der Kreig ist vorüber*" (What's up youngster, the war is over). I had then to 'seize' the ship's documents and hoist the White Ensign with the Marines drawn to attention, and afterwards stay on board until the ship reached the other end of the Kiel Canal. I got to know the canal rather well. I was supposed to look out for suspicious activity and to overhear conversations. All these rituals could have been viewed as reasonable precautions at the time, but it was soon apparent that it was a bit of a sham and no resistance ever occurred. So far as taking note of any conversations with me or between the crew, this would have required someone who knew *Plattdeutsch*, or low German, with which I was entirely unfamiliar. It was only some years later that the Navy calculated the funds received from selling off the captured merchant ships and, for the very last time, distributed prize money to officers and men. There was some controversy about who should receive it, and there were those that grudge the inclusion of RAF Coastal Command in the division of spoils. I did not venture any claim based on the tonnage that I had formally seized in prize. What I did receive, round about 1952 or so, in the light of my service and seniority was £15.10s which Margaret and I blew on a visit to Covent Garden opera; and in those days it paid for seats in the best stalls!

But as the years slipped by, there were fewer and fewer reminders of being a former naval person, except occasional and very pleasant meetings with Victor, who embarked on the rigorous training leading to his becoming a psychoanalyst. I think we both regretted that we did not see more of each other and it was a great shock, after not seeing him for a year or so, to discover that he had died in his late fifties. The test of the falling away of the past is in one's dreams. I remember asking the eminent German refugee lawyer, Kahn-Freund, one of my senior colleagues at the LSE, whether he dreamt in German or English, with his excellent command of English but strong German accent. He had every right to be put out by this piece of cheek, but, taking his time, told me that English had taken over much more quickly than he realised would happen. The point of my query was my own experience in ceasing to dream about the sea very quickly, but the lack of control over the content of one's dreams makes it risky to believe that the grip of the sea will not return, more so because of writing about it after so many years.

There were later reminders of the deeply ingrained effect of being at sea. When I was Professor of Economics at Edinburgh (1957-62), I was produced at a lunch given to a naval captain who was hoping to establish a naval unit at the university. He enquired about my service career and revealed that we had met before – he had been a member of the Court of Enquiry held in Devonport Barracks after the 'Tunnel' disaster and recalled my deep disappointment at the misuse of the Y information which might have saved lives. Later, when Principal of the University of Buckingham, I was visited by the titular ruler of the Isle of Man, the Lieutenant Governor, with whom we were in negotiation over the award of education grants for Manx students who wished to study with us. He was an ex-Admiral, but we discovered that many years before he had been a midshipman on HMS *Anson* when Victor and I had been temporary members of the Gun Room. Our mysterious role had intrigued the 'middies' but some, including himself, remembered our visit with pleasure because Victor and I had helped him and others to write up their logbooks which called for some literary competence.

To celebrate our Golden Wedding, Margaret and I with some close friends sailed on the famous packet boat from Bergen up the Norwegian Coast and as far as Kirkenes, taking in places that I associated with German aircraft landing strips, Tromso Fjord where the *Tirpitz* had finally been sunk, the North Cape and to Kirkenes from whence we had helped to evacuate those who had fled from its incineration by the German troops. The next port, Vadsø, also suffered a similar fate. It incorporates a splendid small 18th Century fort where this event is not forgotten. I suppose to put the many German visitors at their ease it records that the Germans were not the first to set it alight. The previous incendiarists had been the Royal Navy – but that was a little time previously – during the Napoleonic Wars!

Again, only a year ago, my wife and I sold our apartment in Edinburgh. Following the usual practice after the sale was agreed, we were visited by the buyers, an elderly couple like ourselves, who were expected to inspect our property in detail and to agree on the retention or otherwise of items of furniture. From his bearing and countenance I risked asking the husband if he had served at sea. Yes, and moreover we discovered that he had been Asdic Officer on HMS *Jamaica* on both the trips that Victor and I made to Spitzbergen! His wife had difficulty getting him to complete the inspection for we became deeply engaged in reminiscences during which he made a spirited defence of Captain Hughes-Hallett, whose disciplinary code had surprised Victor and myself!

Every serviceman, I suspect, can tell similar stories about the reminders of their past, but I have one more which is perhaps a little unusual. In early 1992 I was asked by the United Nations to head a Mission to the Russian Federation which was to advise on the social dimension of policies which would have to be developed as a complement to the extensive changes in the running of the economy. It was a hurried visit to provide briefing material for Boris Yeltsin, only recently installed as President of the Federation and about to visit the USA and the United Nations. Protocol required that we discussed the Federation's problems with high-level politicians and officials, usually over lunch, and one of these occasions was hosted by the then Minister of the Interior, Mr Yerin. We faced each other across the lunch table, shook hands and he asked the usual question – was this my first visit to Russia? No? Then you have been in Moskva before? No. Not Moskva, Murmansk. (That was not strictly correct, though it made a good riposte and, anyway, Murmansk was where the merchant ships of convoys docked, if not their escort.) I added, jocularly, that the Soviet Government had struck a medal for the brave sailors who had sailed the vasty deep of the Arctic, that the award had been extended to British sailors but that I had never received one. He was obviously a little put out, though I had tried very hard to make it clear that I was not complaining. Mr Yerin snapped his fingers, whispered in the ear of a young official who had been rushed to his side and the latter abruptly disappeared. Shortly after I returned home, I received a large envelope containing an impressive certificate signed by the Chairman of the Soviet Committee of War Veterans, commending my war service. But that was not all. About a year later, the Ministry of Defence sent me a letter enclosing the brightly coloured Soviet medal. The medal came with a stern message from the Ministry of Defence. I was never to wear it alongside British awards on official occasions.

The Proscribed Medal

Советский комитет ветеранов войны

SOVIET COMMITTEE   OF WAR VETERANS

БЛАГОДАРНОСТЬ

SIR   ALAN   PEACOCK

THIS IS TO ACKNOWLEDGE OUR APPRECIATION

OF YOUR OUTSTANDING COURAGE AND PERSONAL

CONTRIBUTION TO THE ALLIED SUPPORT

OF THE SOVIET PEOPLE WHO FOUGHT FOR

FREEDOM AGAINST NAZI GERMANY.

Председатель
Советского комитета ветеранов войны
Герой Советского Союза
маршал авиации

Chairman   А. СИЛАНТЬЕВ

Ответственный секретарь
Советского комитета ветеранов войны

Secretary   А. МАЛОВ

14 - February 1992г.

Tovarich Pavlin (Peacock) receives his due recognition

Chapter 8

RETROSPECT

——

The Grip of the Past

The traces of the past which tug at one's sleeve from time to time leave another legacy in the form of one's conduct and attitudes which are difficult to erase, more so than subsequent experiences, however deep and memorable. As the years go by, the tug gives way to a firm grip, and the memories of a 'former naval person', though inevitably selective make one ponder on the significance of having been spared to tell the tale and induced to explore its meaning. Anyone surviving active service can pinpoint the influences of their service career on their future attitudes and behaviour and express them in many different ways. What I try to do is to isolate those influences which are the direct result of being an eavesdropper, for otherwise I would only be adding little to the countless observations of my generation of veterans. I know that success in doing so is not guaranteed because being a sailor of sorts as well as being regarded as some sort of boffin produces a commingling of experiences which have both left their mark.

Reconciliation

Beginning with the immediacy of war, one's very situation where the enemy is not directly confronted means that he becomes an abstraction. One never actually came face to face with a German matelot or airman. One was not looking for the 'whites of their eyes' to take aim and shoot to kill. In the midst of the mountainous seas and atrocious cold, our imagination of what the 'bastards' were like and what we believed they deserved led only to mutual sympathy with their condition and the possible fate of being frozen to death if sunk and forced to abandon ship; for there was nowhere to hide, no escape. Of course, in other theatres of war there were horrific stories about sailors being shot while attempting to avoid drowning, but these were balanced by others in which the enemy behaved with remarkable generosity.

The only German sailor whom I met who had served in the Arctic was the unfortunate last captain of the *Tirpitz*, Konter-Admiral Peters. He had been retired just before the end of the war and lived in Ekernförde, nor far from Kiel. When at Kiel I was sent with a naval engineer to interview him about the final days of his battleship and to find out which methods of attack we had used were the most successful. It could not have been easy for him to go over these events and he not only behaved with dignity and courtesy but tactfully helped me in translating German naval engineering terms into English. There was no hint in his bearing and discourse to suggest that he was ingratiating himself with his conquerors – hardly likely in being faced with a 23 year old conscript five rungs below him in the ladder of ranks.

I admit that I did not have the same feeling of respect in meeting a U-boat officer of my own age some time later, when I acted as a tutor at Wilton Park. He was an out-and-out Nazi and a regular officer, now a prisoner and his career in ruins. We all but spat at one another, but he decided that it was in his interests to acquire a good knowledge of English. He worked hard at it, and tested me thoroughly in my tutorials on the meaning of words and expressions which he did not understand. One day he asked me in his usual serious manner what was the meaning of the word 'f--------g'. I regarded this as a try-on and simply said that he knew perfectly well what it meant, given its similarity to the German equivalent. No, he protested – he was not pulling my leg. He wanted to understand its meaning in 'zis context – ja, zis context' – I ask a British soldier ze time and he says: 'it's 'alf past f--------g twelve mate'. I gave up trying to find an equivalent German form of interpolation.

An abstraction is too strong a description of one's perception of the enemy when engaged in long-distance spying. During hostilities, it was difficult not to admit that, like those who engaged in dangerous spying activities out in the cold, one developed a kind of affinity with those whom we hoped would supply us with information which we could use to frustrate their intentions. Even if we only overheard their W/T signals in code, one developed a 'guest list' of operators who exerted a certain amount of individuality in their transmissions. One could only admire the courage and endurance of the crews of weather planes making daily flights across the vast emptiness of the Arctic and regretted that we could not have any reservations about decoding their messages which could affect our own survival.

I was put to the test of reconciliation almost as soon as I became a lecturer in economics at the LSE in 1948 because included in the list of overseas scholars was a young German, Herbert Giersch, Dozent at Munster University, and the first German academic economist to be supported by the British Council in their efforts to re-establish academic ties with West Germany. He had been a junior U-boat Officer towards the end of WW2 and a prisoner of war at Haltwhistle, where he had studied English. A simple calculation of our ages removed one barrier because neither of us belonged to a generation which had had a say in the governance of our countries during the crucial 1930s years. Our naval experiences as conscripts entailed no animosity, more the contrary as we recalled our reactions to being temporary matelots. Professional interests coincided and we were both initially 'outside' observers of a completely different academic tradition at LSE in which there was no rigid hierarchy of the kind we had both been used to. This was the beginning of a long and lasting professional collaboration and friendship of over fifty years, during which Herbert has emerged as one of the leading figures in German academic and public life. Our junior colleagues have little idea, one suspects, of the healing process, often long and painful, which is a legacy of total war and think it entirely natural that their ancient forbears, such as Herbert and myself, should be friends. German and British economists at the conference table of seminars are usually indistinguishable , a consequence no doubt of the formers' excellent command of English, and national differences which presage the possibility of another conflict of the sort that Herbert and I were engaged in never reveal themselves. Long may it remain so.

An Intellectual Legacy

The second permanent influence was the required amount of investment in the techniques of eavesdropping. Not that this was a conscious process. After the basic instruction at Wimbledon and later Cheadle, we were left to benefit from our own experience and initiative. Keeping abreast with military German and W/T procedures was essential but occasionally a wider knowledge of German culture could be useful, a primitive example already given being the German operator with musical interests who thereby helped our decoding. There was nothing structured in the occasional reading of German books, though one was helped by the intelligence staff of Cheadle who had a wide knowledge of the extent to which German education and culture generally impinged on the business of understanding the content of coded messages. There was a much more direct incentive to extend one's technical and general vocabulary when we were all sent to Germany at the end of the European war. When I graduated and became a junior lecturer in Economics at St Andrews, I could draw upon this knowledge in order to become conversant with German and Austrian economic thought when enjoined to offer some lectures on the subject. There was an unexpected result. In 1948 I applied for a lectureship at LSE and in the interview was questioned in detail about this interest, notably by Lord Robbins and Friedrich Hayek. My knowledge of German in particular and their, I believe, exaggerated respect for the Scottish tradition of teaching in political economy led them to appoint me to the post. So there is a direct connection between my eavesdropping activities and getting my foot on the ladder of a career. It is not something that could have happened to me otherwise.

Knowledge of languages was once regarded as an essential part of the equipment of training as an economist. This was particularly so at the LSE where before the Second World War the specialist economics syllabuses included reference to works in German and French and sometimes in Italian. A working knowledge of commercial German and French was laid down as part of the examined syllabus of the BSc.(Econ) degree when I joined its staff, but it was not long before it disappeared. By the time I was appointed to my first Chair of Economics at Edinburgh in 1956, a revolution in economics training was already under way. It became much more important to be able to formulate economics hypotheses in mathematical form and to test them with the use of quite sophisticated statistical techniques. Economists ceased primarily to be scholars and those who stuck to the study of the development of economic analysis were frequently suspected of doing so because they could not face up to the rigours of re-training. Although still fascinated and stimulated by what I was able to read in the language which my Naval service had fostered, I fully accepted this need for change. In my inaugural lecture at Edinburgh, I very brashly stated that 'one did not emulate the example of Adam Smith, merely by being an authority on what he had written'. If I had to place my studies in a time frame, then I was not a student of what had happened but what the economic future might bring. I hope I have learnt better.

Again, my 'Y' service had a pronounced bearing on how my professional concerns developed. First of all, I was lucky enough to be engaged in a job requiring the use of one's brains. Making use of corrupt signals, using accumulated knowledge of enemy signal procedures and how these revealed information on their intentions, and formulating some hypothesis about their impact on the progress of an operation, working largely independently of the strict routine of daily naval life at sea, I was saved much of the tedium which causes mental powers to atrophy. Less fortunate colleagues at LSE complained that they had not had the time or inclination to read a book remotely related to their specialism even when they had the enforced leisure to do so during the gaps, often very long ones, between periods of inaction and battles on land and sea.

The second influence was less obvious yet more subtle. Developments in economic thought in the post-war years led to insights into economic behaviour which demonstrated the importance of intelligence in all kinds of transactions involving exchanges, including the production, sale and demand for information itself. The incentive to sellers to provide correct information to buyers and compensation if their information proved to be false clearly depends on the degree of competition between them. If the goods or services are continually in demand, then dissatisfied buyers can switch suppliers. In fact, continuous exchanges provide evidence of greater satisfaction on both sides of the transaction than would otherwise be the case if no sale took place. The strategy of each side of the bargain is to seek co-operation. This is why economists have become deeply involved in examining strategy as a manifestation of economic behaviour. Much of what is now called 'game theory' was developed by mathematicians engaged on operational research during WW2 but with military strategy in mind.

However, unlike the competitive market situation which might be described as a 'positive sum, co-operative game', those engaged in fighting one another are at the other extreme of a 'zero-sum, non-co-operative game' in which if one side gains, the other loses. Intelligence work is employed to maximize the gains of one side only, and this means finding out as much as possible about enemy intentions and revealing as little as possible of one's own (including sending forth misleading information) – always subject to whether the cost of obtaining intelligence is less than its perceived benefits. Although I have never become a specialist in game theory, I realised early in its introduction into economics that it offered very useful insights into economic behaviour and as I was then lecturing at LSE on theories of price formation I volunteered to give a presentation of its essential elements to Lionel Robbins' staff seminar. I found myself recalling my Arctic experiences as a guide to the kind of situations about which game theory might enlighten us.

The reader may more readily appreciate this example of the way in which one's intellectual past maintains its hold on one's interests and expertise by this simple formulation of what I shall call 'Admiral Moore's Dilemma'. Let's go back to the decision that Admiral Moore had to take given the expectation that there was a high probability that his force would be sighted by enemy aircraft. The force would be sighted or not sighted. To avoid being sighted, the command could be given to shoot down or not to shoot down the sighting aircraft. The consequences of either of these actions can be shown in what game theorists would call a Pay Off Matrix:

Response	Sighting	No Sighting
Shoot Down	-	?
Not Shoot Down	0	+

- means the worst possible outcome.
? means uncertainty of outcome depending on ability of the enemy to deduce presence of hostile forces.
0 means uncertainty about enemy interpretation of Admiral Moore's evasive action by altering course, if sighting takes place.
+ enemy unaware of presence of force, also made possible by evasive action.

This stark form is quite a useful way of clarifying one's ideas about what courses are open to one, but, as with many game theory examples, the strategist may only see it as a starting point for setting out ideas about which action is appropriate. In the case of Admiral Moore, this short-term situation was clear enough and he was locked in to a game he had to play. When not bound by the stark choices that are so often found in war, this sort of example invites the speculation that with a range of choices need one enter the game in the first place, and can't the players learn from experience and seek to alter its rules? I leave to the reader's imagination the games that can be played with the theory of games as a way of forecasting the probable outcome of complicated and continuous bargaining in both commercial and international relations.

Personal History Repeats Itself – Almost

So in a curious way, family personal history has repeated itself. The horrors of World War I which my father had to live with were counterbalanced by the opportunity afforded him to apply his knowledge as an entomologist to the problems of trench fever. His published work in this area was a contributory factor to his being appointed to a Chair at University College, Dundee in 1926 where he remained active for thirty years. I in my turn had similar if not such horrifying experiences as he had witnessed and also had the opportunity of capitalising on what I learnt, though both of us would have been reluctant to support the proposition that war is also some kind of purifying experience. I have also explained how my father made every effort after WW1 to make friends with those who had been enemies.

But there was one important difference. My father like many of his colleagues of similar age was much less inclined to repeat the process of reconciliation after WW2, having suffered the disillusionment brought about by the willing acceptance of Nazi doctrines by German contemporaries. My senior colleagues at LSE fully understood this and they like him would have little to do with Germans and Austrians of their own generation or at least became very selective in their choice of those they were prepared to meet when the war in Europe ended. Not surprisingly, neither my father nor my mother ever returned to Germany.

Epilogue

THE ENIGMATIC SAILOR

———

After consulting the Naval Historical Branch of the Ministry of Defence, who have been immensely helpful to me, I decided out of curiosity to request the Ministry for a copy of my service record, but also because it might contain information which would enable me to check on some of my dimming recollections. I had assumed that the record could be quite detailed and might include opinions expressed about one's attainments and failures. I was particularly curious about the decision to award me a decoration to which I thought I was barely entitled. I was, however, warned by the Naval Historical Branch that access was not a right and a record would not enter the public domain until sixty years after the cessation of an individual's service. This is a reasonable protection against misuse of an individual record obtained by false pretences and which might damage the individual concerned.

I tracked down the Defence Record 2A branch to somewhere in Hayes, Middlesex and wrote a letter in July 2001 stating the reasons for my request. A Mrs Herbert wrote me a polite letter pointing out, to my surprise, that her 'small busy section' received between 3500 and 5000 enquiries a year and priority, understandably, had to be given to welfare and benefit enquiries, but I ought to obtain a reply within 40 days – a good biblical measure of justifiable delay – and to write again if this presented any difficulties (which clearly it did not).

Well within the 40 days I received a sheet of paper typed on both sides, whereas I suppose that, like many misguided souls, I was expecting the contents of a file. It recorded service on two ships to which I had been seconded from *Woolston* but which I had never stepped aboard. My grandiose title of Navigator's Yeoman had become 'Chart Corrector'. I was credited with a degree in German which I did not possess. There was no record of any of the ships on which I had served in the Arctic, the only 'ship' given being *Proserpine*, the stone frigate. There was no record of a Wound and Hurt Certificate. The citation for the DSC was given but no background information on the reasons for the award, which would be difficult to justify if I had been ashore during my Arctic service. No assessment of my performance at any stage of my career was included.

I wrote to Mrs Herbert pointing out that, leaving aside my surprise at the paucity of information, the 'bare bones' information was wrong in certain respects. While she was very sympathetic, and kindly remarked that 'it is always nice to know more of the story', she made it clear that no corrections were permissible. What is stated in the record is what happened and what is not there did not happen. Or supposedly could not be revealed, I wondered? That made me hesitate but what I have revealed is only adding what I hope is a touch of colour to official accounts of intelligence work. In any case, I did not think that I could make a case for pressing for further personal information which would expand or correct my narrative, and how long would I have to wait before clearance could be given, if that were necessary? I do know that a large quantity of naval records no longer exists including, I have been informed, the log books of ships that might have contained reference to our efforts.

The enigma of my naval career has followed me around for many years and, when I became a university Vice-Chancellor it led to the rumour that during WW2 I had been a spy! So the bare official record of my doings offers some justification for attempting to remove 'the stigma of enigma' by adding a fair amount of flesh to the bare bones of the official account of my service. Nevertheless it would be churlish not to express my gratitude to the Ministry of Defence for omitting from it any mention of the criminal offence of missing my ship at Rosyth!

Appendix

THE LANDLUBBERS LEARN THE LINGO

———

A young wartime recruit to the Royal Navy would soon have become familiar with a string of strange words many of them terms which go back to the days of Nelson. Arriving at the gate of a training establishment he would be surprised to find that it was already designated as a 'ship' though firmly on dry land, such as HMS *Royal Arthur*. One such word might not be entirely unknown to some:

> SPROG. *A new recruit, a term also used in the Royal Air Force, the equivalent army term being a 'rookie'.*

But why is the 'ship' referred to by the old salts as a 'stone frigate'?

> STONE FRIGATE. *A frigate is a very old term for a class of sailing vessel in many navies and now used as a general term for smaller ships. A Stone Frigate was a rather contemptuous term for a shore-based establishment such as a barracks or training base masquerading under a title which gave the impression that it was a sea-going vessel. Thus the naval base at Rosyth was HMS Cochrane. Those serving in them did not have to suffer the discomforts and dangers of their sea-going counterparts. However, they tended to adopt*

naval parlance which suggested that they were similarly situated. For example, a sailor seeking to go off-duty would seek 'permission to go ashore' and, if granted, would 'go over the side' even though he might merely be going through the dockyard gate, down the street and into the nearest pub.

On being issued with his naval uniform and kit he might be lucky and receive a nice smile from the issuer who could be a

WREN. *A colloquial term for a member of the Women's Royal Naval Service (WRNS).*

(Wrens are no longer confined to shore duties and, as I write this, are on ships called to action in case we go to war with Iraq.)

If he gets into some sort of trouble such as late back from local 'shore leave' he might find himself confronted by a

MASTER-AT-ARMS. *The Chief Petty Officer in a base or on a ship responsible to the officer commanding for enforcement of discipline – a naval policeman, much feared and respected. He is to this day still called by the slang term of JAUNTY which goes back to Nelson's time – originating from the French* gendarme.

who will have at his side a

REGULATING PETTY OFFICER *a member of the 'ship's' police whom he must learn to identify in the colourful language of regular sailors as the CRUSHER.*

Perhaps with a 'sprog' their bark would be worse than their bite, and there would also be one person to whom he might turn if put on a charge who might intercede. That would be the

SIN BO'SUN. *A jocular term for a naval padre, Bo'sun being short for BOATSWAIN – we shall meet this interesting petty officer later. Sin is of obvious professional interest to the holder of the title. The less colourful term in the RAF was Sky Pilot.*

He would soon notice that the rank of officers could be identified by the number of braid rings on the cuffs of their jackets and to watch out for the

STRAIGHT RINGERS. *Regular officers as distinct from HOs (q.v.) were recognizable by straight rings. This distinguished them from mere wartime sailors who had wavy rings and therefore known as the Wavy Navy or as Saturday Night Sailors. Normally a naval base of any size would be commanded by a senior straight ringer, sometimes brought out of retirement.*

Which leads naturally to defining

'HOs' – *short for 'hostilities only' and accordingly used to describe those who volunteered or were called up to serve for the duration of the war only, as distinct from career naval officers. It includes reservists who had contracted to return for wartime service.*

When undergoing initial training, during which a sprog would be identified as suitable for specialist training in some branch of the service, e.g. telegraphist or signalman, there would be a few who were picked out as

CW CANDIDATES *deemed suitable to undergo training to become officers, and hence to hold His Majesty's Commission.*

Normally ratings on joining a ship would encounter further unfamiliar and sometimes colourful terms with which to be able to hold an ordinary conversation with shipmates, not to mention impress their girl friends ashore. Here are those that appear in my narrative.

On boarding a destroyer for the first time, the sprog would report to the COXSWAIN *–usually a Chief Petty Officer (CPO), or petty officer (PO), who was the senior helmsman. He would always take the helm when in action and in very stormy weather.*

The Coxswain although exercising general supervision over crew would leave the allocation of duties, other than the steering of the ship, to the BOATSWAIN – *the Petty Officer in charge of the assignment of tasks for day-to-day running of the ship and the condition of its equipment, e.g. rigging, anchors, and the ordering of stores.*

The ship's daily routine or special orders are announced by a

BOATSWAIN'S MATE *drawing attention by blowing a curved whistle worn on a lanyard round his neck. The Boatswain's call is also used on ceremonial occasions such as the 'piping aboard' of officers of Flag Rank or visiting dignitaries.*

The two most popular pipes conveyed by the Boatswain's Mate's call were 'Up spirits' and 'Libertymen, fall in' which calls for an explanation of

GROG – *a daily issue of one part rum and three parts water and named after the 18th Century Admiral Vernon known as 'old Grog' who had instituted the practice of dilution. The Officer of the Day was responsible for the issue and in theory each sailor opting for 'G' rather than 'T' (see Chapter 2) was supposed to drink this brew in his presence. In wartime watchkeeping duties could prevent this and each mess would send a representative to draw the rum ration. (Our Officer of the Day certified that the rum had been watered but, apart from a formal baptism with a few drops of water, neat rum was issued. I did not come across Grog in the strict sense until I was temporarily transferred to another destroyer where the correct practice was followed.) The issue of rum was discontinued in 1970.*

As the word 'libertymen' suggests the

LIBERTY BOAT *was the sailor's term for parade and inspection on deck in preparation for permission to go ashore for a short leave of a day or overnight. The term was used irrespective as to whether libertymen required transport from a ship at anchor to the shore, had merely to step off the ship already in harbour or were part of the complement of a 'stone frigate'.*

The steering of the ship follows the orders of the Captain, who on a wartime destroyer could be a Lieutenant Commander, i.e. with two and half rings, usually straight ones. He or the Officer of the Watch would issue steering instructions to the helmsman. A sprog would take his turn at the helm but under the watchful eye of the

QUARTERMASTER – *the senior helmsman responsible to the COXSWAIN who would be at least a Leading Seaman and qualified to take the helm on leaving and entering harbour.*

A less pleasant assignment would be that of cleaning the

> HEADS – *the naval term for the officers' and ratings' lavatories. Originally the Heads were open spaces on both sides of the head of a sailing ship reached by short ladders from the forecastle. In a rough sea it was obviously a hazardous business reaching them and care had to be taken to go down on the lee side of the ship when the wind was blowing hard!*

As I was never trained in gunnery drill, I need not bother the reader with the technical terms associated with it, but I do mention one important piece of weaponry, namely the

> DEPTH CHARGE, *a canister filled with explosive and, in destroyers such as Woolston, fired from projectors on each side and dropped from the stern. The pattern of charges is set to explode at the estimated depth of the U-boat. This limited the older destroyers to attacking a submerged U-boat only after it had passed over it.*

A depth charge was hurled out into the

> DRINK, *the slang term of obvious derivation used for the sea.*

A member of the Lower Deck who, like the author, was ordered to report for training for a Commission became a

> CADET RATING *whose status as one undergoing training for promotion to officer rank was indicated by a white band on his cap while still in rating uniform. It is interesting to note that their army counterparts were designated officer cadets.*

On completing the training successfully and promoted to Temporary Acting Sub-Lieutenant, Royal Naval Volunteer Reserve, the author's transformation was symbolised by being immediately admitted to the

> WARDROOM *the naval term for the officers' mess whether ashore or afloat. All officers, with the exception of the Ship's Captain, would mess in the wardroom although there would be a separate mess entitled the*

GUNROOM *for midshipmen and sub-lieutenants under the age of 23 but only found in larger ships and now abolished.*

The special duties on which the author was engaged requires some knowledge of unfamiliar terms and procedures but these are better explained as they arise. However, there are a few words that occur in the later narrative which do not fit with the chronology of the author's activities and which are not self-explanatory. These include:

DITTY BOX. *Originally a small wooden box issued to sailors to keep their valuables and small personal belongings but replaced during World War II by an undistinguished small cardboard case. Older reservists recalled to duty still possessed ditty boxes.*

WAR WEAPONS WEEKS *were officially approved campaigns to induce citizens to subscribe to war loans. The climax of the week was generally a Services Parade designed to induce the necessary degree of patriotism with a March Past taken by a senior services officer flanked by civic dignitaries.*

SERANG. *A Lascar boatswain. Lascars were Indian sailors and Lascar crews were common on British merchant and troop ships before World War II.*

CIVVY STREET. *Slang expression used generally in the Services for that delectable state of a return to civilian status.*

LINE AHEAD. *The term line is used to denote the formation adopted by warships acting in concert as in cruising exercises and, of course, in battle. In Line Ahead each ship follows the wake of the one in front of her. This was the traditional formation in sailing ship days when guns could only fire broadside. The introduction of guns mounted on turrets and capable of firing in different directions enabled ships to adopt more flexible formations.*